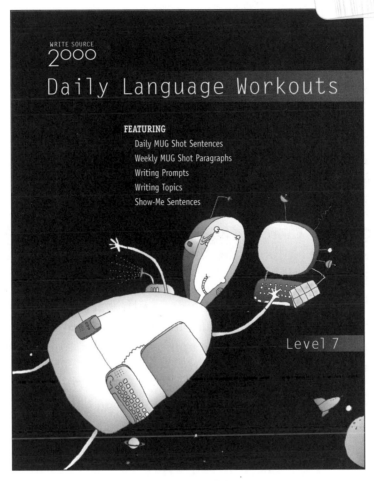

WRITE SOURCE
2000

Daily Language Workouts

FEATURING
Daily MUG Shot Sentences
Weekly MUG Shot Paragraphs
Writing Prompts
Writing Topics
Show-Me Sentences

Level 7

Daily language and writing practice for
Grade 7

WRITE SOURCE®

GREAT SOURCE EDUCATION GROUP
a Houghton Mifflin Company
Wilmington, Massachusetts
www.greatsource.com

A Few Words About
Daily Language Workouts 7

Before you begin . . .

The activities in this book will help your students build basic writing and language skills. You'll find three types of exercises on the following pages:

MUG Shot Sentences There are 175 sentences highlighting **m**echanics, **u**sage, and/or **g**rammar (MUG). There's one for every day of the school year, arranged in 35 weekly groups. Students correct the errors included in each sentence, developing both writing and editing skills in the process.

MUG Shot Paragraphs There are 35 weekly paragraphs. Each paragraph covers many of the same skills as the five daily sentences and serves as a concise review of the week's activities.

Daily Writing Practice This section begins with **writing prompts,** presented on pages that you can photocopy or place on an overhead projector. The prompts include thought-provoking topics and graphics designed to inspire expository, narrative, descriptive, persuasive, and creative writing. There are also lists of intriguing **writing topics.** Finally, the **Show-Me sentences** provide starting points for paragraphs, essays, and a wide variety of other writing forms.

Authors: Pat Sebranek and Dave Kemper

Printed in the United States of America

International Standard Book Number: 0-669-47234-4

3 4 5 6 7 8 9 10 -POO- 04 03 02

Table of Contents

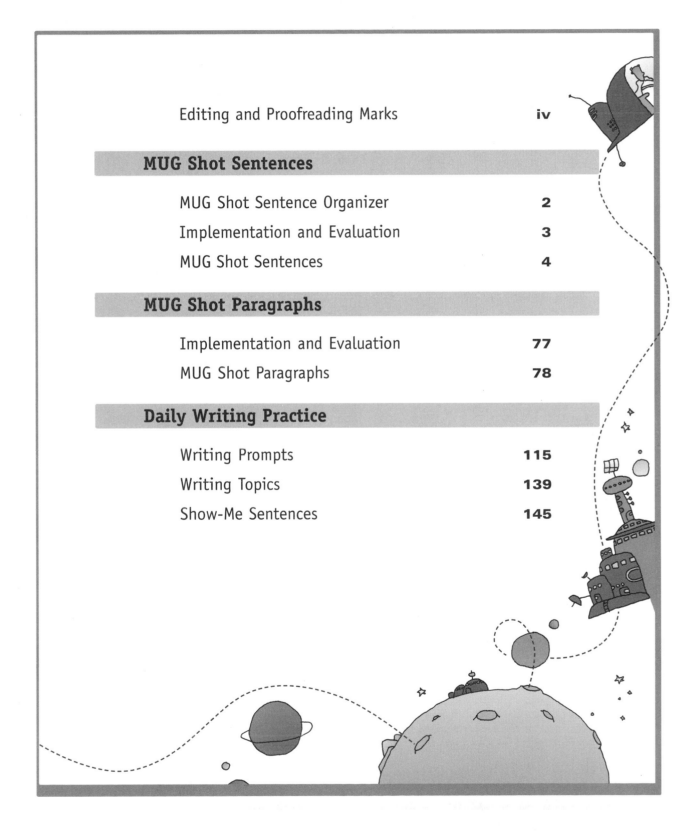

Editing and Proofreading Marks   iv

MUG Shot Sentences

MUG Shot Sentence Organizer   2

Implementation and Evaluation   3

MUG Shot Sentences   4

MUG Shot Paragraphs

Implementation and Evaluation   77

MUG Shot Paragraphs   78

Daily Writing Practice

Writing Prompts   115

Writing Topics   139

Show-Me Sentences   145

Editing and Proofreading Marks

Use these symbols to correct each MUG Shot sentence and paragraph.

Insert here.	∧	*them* take∧home
Insert a comma, semicolon, or colon.	∧, ∧; ∧:	Troy∧,Michigan
Insert a period.	⊙	Mrs⊙
Insert a hyphen or a dash.	∧ ∧	one∧third cup
Insert a question mark or an exclamation point.	?∧ !∧	How about you∧?
Capitalize a letter.	/ (or) ≡	*T*/toronto (or) toronto≡
Make a capital letter lowercase.	/	*h*/History
Replace or delete.	— (or) ℊ	*cold* a ~~hot~~ day (or) a ~~not~~ day *hot* (or) a ~~hot~~ day
Insert an apostrophe or quotation marks.	∨' ∨" ∨"	Bill∨'s ∨"Wow!∨"
Use italics.	_____	Tracker
Insert parentheses.	(∧)∧	letters(∧from A to Z)∧

MUG Shot Sentences

The MUG Shot sentences are designed to be used at the beginning of each class period as a quick and efficient way to review **m**echanics, **u**sage, and **g**rammar. Each sentence can be corrected and discussed in 3 to 5 minutes.

MUG Shot Sentence Organizer   **2**

Implementation and Evaluation   **3**

MUG Shot Sentences   **4**

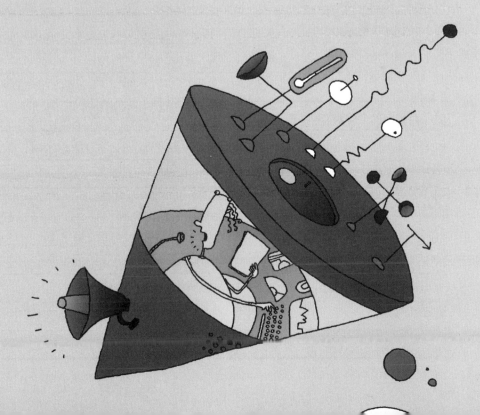

MUG Shot Sentence Organizer

Original Sentence:

Corrected Sentence:

Original Sentence:

Corrected Sentence:

Original Sentence:

Corrected Sentence:

Original Sentence:

Corrected Sentence:

Original Sentence:

Corrected Sentence:

Implementation and Evaluation

There are 35 weeks of daily MUG Shot sentences. The students may use the "Editing and Proofreading Marks" in their handbooks or on page iv of this book to make corrections.

Implementation

On the days that you use MUG Shot sentences, we suggest that you write one or two of them on the board at the beginning of the class period. Allow students time to read each sentence to themselves. (Make sure they understand the sentences.) Then have students correct each MUG Shot in a space reserved for them in their notebooks (or on a copy of the "MUG Shot Sentence Organizer" provided on page 2 of this book). Next, have students discuss their corrections in pairs or as a class. Make sure everyone records the corrections on their papers. And, more importantly, make sure all students understand why the corrections were made.

You may also have students correct the sentences orally. Write the corrections on the board as students provide them. (Use the proofreading marks on page iv.) Have one student explain his or her corrections and discuss the results. Then ask all students to write the corrected form in their notebooks.

Each Friday, review the MUG Shots covered for the week. You might assign the MUG Shot paragraph that contains errors similar to the type students have worked on for the week. (See page 75.)

Note: By design, each page of sentences can be reproduced for student use or made into an overhead transparency.

Evaluation

If you assign sentences daily, evaluate your students' work at the end of each week. We recommend that you give them a basic performance score for their daily work. This performance score might be based on having each sentence for that week correctly written in their language arts notebooks (before or after any discussion).

You can also use the weekly paragraphs to evaluate student progress. The paragraphs cover the same kinds of errors as the sentences, so students should be able to cover a good percentage of these errors.

WEEK 1: Potpourri

■ **Sentence Fragment, Capitalization**

Athens, a city in greece named after athena, the greek goddess of war and wisdom.

■ **Using the Right Word, Run-On Sentence**

In Greek myth, centaurs were half man and half horse apparently, that did not seam totally weird too people back than.

■ **Capitalization, Apostrophe, Adjective (Articles)**

In japan its considered good luck to cross the path of an black cat.

■ **Numbers, Comma (Interjections), End Punctuation**

Wow people in the world drink more than 260,000,000 glasses of soda every day

■ **Quotation Marks, Comma (Appositives), Subject-Verb Agreement**

Aesop the writer of such famous fables as The Fox and the Grapes were a Greek slave.

WEEK 1: Corrected Sentences

■ **Sentence Fragment, Capitalization**

Athens, is a city in <u>G</u>reece named after <u>A</u>thena, the <u>G</u>reek goddess of war

and wisdom.

■ **Using the Right Word, Run-On Sentence**

In Greek myth, centaurs were half man and half horse. Apparently, that

did not ~~seam~~ *seem* totally weird ~~too~~ *to* people back ~~than~~ *then*.

■ **Capitalization, Apostrophe, Adjective (Articles)**

In <u>J</u>apan it's considered good luck to cross the path of ~~an~~ *a* black cat.

■ **Numbers, Comma (Interjections), End Punctuation**

Wow, people in the world drink more than ~~260,000,000~~ *260 million* glasses of soda

every day!

■ **Quotation Marks, Comma (Appositives), Subject-Verb Agreement**

Aesop, the writer of such famous fables as "The Fox and the Grapes," ~~were~~ *was*

a Greek slave.

WEEK 2: A Medley

■ **Subject-Verb Agreement, Adjective (Comparative/Superlative), Verb (Irregular)**

It don't seem possible that Beethoven could have wrote many of his most fine symphonies after going deaf.

■ **Verb (Irregular), Double Subject, Plurals**

Mozart he begun writing symphonys when he was five years old.

■ **Comma (Appositives and To Separate Phrases and Clauses), Capitalization, Verb (Tense)**

According to legend king arthur becomes king when he pulled the magic sword Excalibur from a stone.

■ **Adjective (Comparative/Superlative), Capitalization, End Punctuation**

Is exxon the most large corporation in america

■ **Abbreviations, Verb (Irregular), Capitalization, Hyphen**

My brother in law knowed all about WW I and WW II after taking history 101.

WEEK 2: Corrected Sentences

- ## Subject-Verb Agreement, Adjective (Comparative/Superlative), Verb (Irregular)

It ~~don't~~ *doesn't* seem possible that Beethoven could have ~~wrote~~ *written* many of his ~~most~~ *finest* ~~fine~~ symphonies after going deaf.

- ## Verb (Irregular), Double Subject, Plurals

Mozart ~~he~~ ~~begun~~ *began* writing ~~symphonys~~ *symphonies* when he was five years old.

- ## Comma (Appositives and To Separate Phrases and Clauses), Capitalization, Verb (Tense)

According to legend, *K*ing *A*rthur ~~becomes~~ *became* king when he pulled the magic sword, Excalibur, from a stone.

- ## Adjective (Comparative/Superlative), Capitalization, End Punctuation

Is *E*xxon the ~~most large~~ *largest* corporation in *A*merica?

- ## Abbreviations, Verb (Irregular), Capitalization, Hyphen

My brother-in-law ~~knowed~~ *knew* all about ~~WW~~ *World War* I and ~~WW~~ *World War* II after taking *H*istory 101.

WEEK 3: Bigger, Higher, Faster, and Me

■ **Verb (Irregular), Apostrophe (Possessives), Spelling**

My heart sinked when I heard the judge anounce my opponents name
as the winner.

■ **Using the Right Word, Comma (Addresses), Plurals, Period**

The record for the quickest, natural berth of triplets is held by Mrs
James Duck of Memphis Tennessee who's three babys arrived in three
minutes!

■ **Numbers, Hyphen (Single-Thought Adjectives), Comma Splice**

Jim Carrey is one of the highest paid entertainers, he earns more than
10,000,000 dollars per movie.

■ **Adjective (Articles and Comparative/Superlative), Abbreviations**

The most large airport in the world is the Saudi Arabian King Khalid
International, which covers a area of 86 sq. mi.

■ **Comma (Addresses), Capitalization, Apostrophe (Possessives)**

aunt juanitas address is 230 pleasant lane oceanview california.

WEEK 3: Corrected Sentences

■ **Verb (Irregular), Apostrophe (Possessives), Spelling**

My heart ~~sinked~~ *sank* when I heard the judge ~~anounce~~ *announce* my opponent's name

as the winner.

■ **Using the Right Word, Comma (Addresses), Plurals, Period**

The record for the quickest, natural ~~berth~~ *birth* of triplets is held by Mrs.

James Duck of Memphis, Tennessee, ~~who's~~ *whose* three ~~babys~~ *babies* arrived in three

minutes!

■ **Numbers, Hyphen (Single-Thought Adjectives), Comma Splice**

Jim Carrey is one of the highest-paid entertainers; (or). He earns more than

$10,000,000 ~~dollars~~ per movie.

■ **Adjective (Articles and Comparative/Superlative), Abbreviations**

The ~~most large~~ *largest* airport in the world is the Saudi Arabian King Khalid

International, which covers ~~a~~ *an* area of 86 ~~sq. mi.~~ *square miles.*

■ **Comma (Addresses), Capitalization, Apostrophe (Possessives)**

Aunt Juanita's address is 230 Pleasant Lane, Oceanview, California.

WEEK 4: I was just wondering . . .

■ **Abbreviations, Using the Right Word, Wordy Sentence, End Punctuation**

Did the biggest baby that ever was born way in at 22 lb. and 8 oz

■ **Comma (Interjections), Apostrophe, End Punctuation**

Man Im happy its finally raining, arent you

■ **Capitalization, Comma (Addresses)**

a. r. wilson of west sussex england owned the oldest goldfish, named fred,

which lived to be 41 years old.

■ **Capitalization, Verb (Tense), Rambling Sentence**

Amelia Earhart grew up in kansas and she was the first woman to fly

solo across the atlantic and in the late 1930s, she disappears while flying

around the world.

■ **Capitalization, Abbreviations, Numbers, Subject-Verb Agreement**

in the U.S., our president receive a salary of 200,000 dollars per year.

WEEK 4: Corrected Sentences

- ## Abbreviations, Using the Right Word, Wordy Sentence, End Punctuation

Did the biggest baby ~~that~~ ever ~~was~~ born ~~way~~ in at 22 ~~lb.~~ and 8 ~~oz~~ *weigh* *pounds ounces?*

- ## Comma (Interjections), Apostrophe, End Punctuation

Man, I'm happy it's finally raining, aren't you?

- ## Capitalization, Comma (Addresses)

A. J. Wilson of West Sussex, England, owned the oldest goldfish, named Fred,

which lived to be 41 years old.

- ## Capitalization, Verb (Tense), Rambling Sentence

Amelia Earhart grew up in Kansas, and She was the first woman to fly

solo across the Atlantic, and In the late 1930s, she ~~disappears~~ *disappeared* while flying

around the world.

- ## Capitalization, Abbreviations, Numbers, Subject-Verb Agreement

In the ~~U.S.,~~ *United States* our president ~~receive~~ *receives* a salary of $200,000 ~~dollars~~ per year.

WEEK 5: Early American History

■ **Comma (To Separate Phrases and Clauses), Capitalization, Misplaced Modifier**

columbus discovered america sailing West from spain in 1492 while trying to reach india.

■ **Using the Right Word, Subject-Verb Agreement**

Before Europeans settled in America, their was more than one million Native Americans living hear.

■ **Abbreviations, Using the Right Word**

The first Europeans to settle in Amer. were the Puritans, whom came hear for religious reasons.

■ **Comma (To Separate Phrases and Clauses), Capitalization, Verb (Tense)**

to protest unfair taxes american revolutionaries throw three shiploads of tea into boston harbor in 1773.

■ **Verb (Irregular), Wordy Sentence, Using the Right Word**

On Christmas Eve 1776, George Washington gone across the Delaware River and lead a surprise attack against the British that caught them unaware.

WEEK 5: Corrected Sentences

■ **Comma (To Separate Phrases and Clauses), Capitalization, Misplaced Modifier**

*C*olumbus discovered *A*merica ~~sailing West from spain~~ in 1492 while *sailing west from Spain,* trying

to reach *I*ndia.

■ **Using the Right Word, Subject-Verb Agreement**

Before Europeans settled in America, ~~their was~~ *there were* more than one million

Native Americans living ~~hear~~. *here*

■ **Abbreviations, Using the Right Word**

The first Europeans to settle in ~~Amer.~~ *America* were the Puritans, ~~whom~~ *who* came

~~hear~~ *here* for religious reasons.

■ **Comma (To Separate Phrases and Clauses), Capitalization, Verb (Tense)**

*T*o protest unfair taxes, *A*merican revolutionaries ~~throw~~ *threw* three shiploads of

tea into *B*oston *H*arbor in 1773.

■ **Verb (Irregular), Wordy Sentence, Using the Right Word**

On Christmas Eve 1776, George Washington ~~gone~~ *went* across the Delaware

River and ~~lead~~ *led* a surprise attack against the British. ~~that caught them~~

~~unaware.~~

WEEK 6: In the 1800s

■ **Numbers, Spelling, Subject-Verb Agreement**

By the 1820s, the avrage American were drinking 7 gallons of pure

alkahol every year.

■ **Plurals, Verb (Irregular), Abbreviations**

In 1835, Oberlin College becomed the 1st college to admit woman.

■ **Using the Right Word, End Punctuation, Run-On Sentence**

Nat Turner, a slave and preacher, lead a slave revolt in 1831 beside 60

white Virginians, 20 black slaves also dyed

■ **Capitalization, Verb (Tense), Spelling**

The Mexican-american war ended in 1848, and the United States gains

525,000 square miles of terratory from mexico.

■ **Comma Splice, Verb (Tense), Using the Right Word, Comma (Interruptions)**

Early in the Civil War, African Americans from the North tried too

enlist, the Union army however rejects them at first.

WEEK 6: Corrected Sentences

- **Numbers, Spelling, Subject-Verb Agreement**

  average *was* *seven*
  By the 1820s, the ~~avrage~~ American ~~were~~ drinking ~~7~~ gallons of pure

  alcohol
  ~~alkahol~~ every year.

- **Plurals, Verb (Irregular), Abbreviations**

  became *first* *women*
  In 1835, Oberlin College ~~becomed~~ the ~~1st~~ college to admit ~~woman~~.

- **Using the Right Word, End Punctuation, Run-On Sentence**

  led *besides*
  Nat Turner, a slave and preacher, ~~lead~~ a slave revolt in 1831; ~~beside~~ 60

  died
  white Virginians, 20 black slaves also ~~dyed~~.

- **Capitalization, Verb (Tense), Spelling**

  A W *gained*
  The Mexican-american war ended in 1848, and the United States ~~gains~~

  territory M
  525,000 square miles of ~~terratory~~ from mexico.

- **Comma Splice, Verb (Tense), Using the Right Word, Comma (Interruptions)**

  to
  Early in the Civil War, African Americans from the North tried ~~too~~

  ⟍(or)⊙T *rejected*
  enlist; the Union army, however, ~~rejects~~ them at first.

WEEK 7: At the Turn of the Century

■ **Comma (Interruptions), Capitalization, Quotation Marks**

my History teacher said, in the civil war, two men died of disease

unfortunately for every soldier killed in battle.

■ **Capitalization, Comma Splice**

hiram Revels was the first African American senator, he was the

Mississippi republican senator from 1870 to 1871.

■ **Using the Right Word, Numbers**

More then 25,000,000 emigrants entered the United States between 1870

and 1916.

■ **Verb (Irregular), Capitalization, Spelling**

in 1927, Charles Lindbergh flyed the first solo flight acrost the Atlantic

ocean.

■ **Spelling, Using the Right Word, Parallelism, Adjective (Articles)**

At the turn of the cenchury, the average laborer got up early each day,

was working 60 hours a week, and maid about 20 cents a hour.

WEEK 7: Corrected Sentences

■ **Comma (Interruptions), Capitalization, Quotation Marks**

My History teacher said, "in the civil war, two men died of disease
, unfortunately, for every soldier killed in battle."

■ **Capitalization, Comma Splice**

Hiram Revels was the first African American senator, he was the
Mississippi republican senator from 1870 to 1871.

■ **Using the Right Word, Numbers**

than 25 million immigrants
More then 25,000,000 emigrants entered the United States between 1870
and 1916.

■ **Verb (Irregular), Capitalization, Spelling**

flew   across
In 1927, Charles Lindbergh flyed the first solo flight acrost the Atlantic
Ocean.

■ **Spelling, Using the Right Word, Parallelism, Adjective (Articles)**

century
At the turn of the cenchury, the average laborer got up early each day,
worked   made   an
was working 60 hours a week, and maid about 20 cents a hour.

WEEK 8: The Twentieth Century

■ **Comma (To Separate Phrases and Clauses), Apostrophe (Possessives), Capitalization, Italics and Underlining**

If you'd like a young peoples reference book read The world almanac for kids 2000.

■ **Using the Right Word, Comma (Dates), Plurals, Comma Splice**

The 19th Amendment was proposed on June 4 1919, it was ratified on August 18 1920 and gave woman the rite too vote.

■ **Comma (Series), Run-On Sentence**

In the 1920s, it was illegal to buy sell or drink alcohol this was called Prohibition.

■ **Capitalization, Comma (To Separate Phrases and Clauses), Spelling**

at the hight of the great depression about 13 million americans were out of work.

■ **Comma (Appositives), Period, Using the Right Word, Capitalization**

franklin d roosevelt the only president to be elected for terms in office was crippled buy Polio.

WEEK 8: Corrected Sentences

- ## Comma (To Separate Phrases and Clauses), Apostrophe (Possessives), Capitalization, Italics and Underlining

  If you'd like a young peoples' reference book, read The world Almanac for
  Kids 2000.

- ## Using the Right Word, Comma (Dates), Plurals, Comma Splice

  The 19th Amendment was proposed on June 4, 1919. It was ratified on
  August 18, 1920, and gave women the right to vote.

- ## Comma (Series), Run-On Sentence

  In the 1920s, it was illegal to buy, sell, or drink alcohol; (or). This was called
  Prohibition.

- ## Capitalization, Comma (To Separate Phrases and Clauses), Spelling

  At the height of the Great Depression, about 13 million Americans were
  out of work.

- ## Comma (Appositives), Period, Using the Right Word, Capitalization

  Franklin D. Roosevelt, the only president to be elected four terms in office,
  was crippled by Polio.

WEEK 9: Recent American History

■ **Using the Right Word, Comma (To Separate Phrases and Clauses), Pronoun-Antecedent Agreement**

Among 1959 and 1962 over 200,000 Cubans immigrated from his homeland.

■ **Capitalization, Comma Splice, End Punctuation, Spelling**

john f. kennedy was the youngest man ever elected as president, he was

the fourth american president to be asassinated

■ **Comma (Dates and Unnecessary), Italics and Underlining, Numbers**

On March 24 1989 the supertanker, Exxon Valdez spilled over 11,000,000

gallons of oil on the Alaska coast.

■ **Spelling, Comma (Dialogue), Period, Quotation Marks**

Mrs Reyes explaned Don't forget that Mississippi, in 1966, was the last

state to abandon Prohibition.

■ **Capitalization, Adjective (Comparative/Superlative), Verb (Irregular)**

in 1980, ronald reagan becomed the most oldest president ever sworn into

office.

WEEK 9: Corrected Sentences

■ **Using the Right Word, Comma (To Separate Phrases and Clauses), Pronoun-Antecedent Agreement**

Between
~~Among~~ 1959 and 1962, over 200,000 Cubans ~~immigrated~~ *emigrated* from ~~his~~ *their* homeland.

■ **Capitalization, Comma Splice, End Punctuation, Spelling**

J F K
John F. Kennedy was the youngest man ever elected as president. He was *H*
A
the fourth American president to be ~~asassinated.~~ *assassinated*

■ **Comma (Dates and Unnecessary), Italics and Underlining, Numbers**

On March 24, 1989, the supertanker, Exxon Valdez spilled over ~~11,000,000~~ *11 million*

gallons of oil on the Alaska coast.

■ **Spelling, Comma (Dialogue), Period, Quotation Marks**

explained
Mrs. Reyes ~~explaned,~~ "Don't forget that Mississippi, in 1966, was the last

state to abandon Prohibition."

■ **Capitalization, Adjective (Comparative/Superlative), Verb (Irregular)**

I R R became
In 1980, Ronald Reagan ~~becomed~~ the ~~most~~ oldest president ever sworn into

office.

WEEK 10: Animal Oddities

■ **Comma (Series), Comma Splice, Plurals**

Earthworms have no tooths eyes bones or nostrils, it's a wonder they get
around.

■ **Using the Right Word, Quotation Marks, End Punctuation**

Did you know that "wolves carry food to there young by swallowing it
and bringing it up again later"

■ **Using the Right Word, Hyphen (Single-Thought Adjectives), End Punctuation**

Did you no that the ever changing chameleon has a tongue longer then
it's body

■ **Using the Right Word, Pronoun-Antecedent Agreement, Spelling, Comma (Interruptions)**

Chameleons are quite versatile; they can change colar and focus its eyes
independantly. Yes that means they can look in too directions at once.

■ **Comma (Series), Subject-Verb Agreement, Dash**

The giraffe can grow up to 18 feet tall is born with horns and do in
spite of popular belief to the contrary have a voice.

WEEK 10: Corrected Sentences

■ **Comma (Series), Comma Splice, Plurals**

Earthworms have no ~~tooths~~ *teeth*, eyes, bones, or nostrils, it's a wonder they get *(or)* I

around.

■ **Using the Right Word, Quotation Marks, End Punctuation**

Did you know that "wolves carry food to ~~there~~ *their* young by swallowing it

and bringing it up again later"?

■ **Using the Right Word, Hyphen (Single-Thought Adjectives), End Punctuation**

Did you ~~no~~ *know* that the ever-changing chameleon has a tongue longer ~~then~~ *than*

~~it's~~ *its* body?

■ **Using the Right Word, Pronoun-Antecedent Agreement, Spelling, Comma (Interruptions)**

Chameleons are quite versatile; they can change ~~color~~ *color* and focus ~~its~~ *their* eyes

~~independantly~~ *independently*. Yes, that means they can look in ~~too~~ *two* directions at once.

■ **Comma (Series), Subject-Verb Agreement, Dash**

The giraffe can grow up to 18 feet tall, is born with horns, and ~~do~~ *does—* in

spite of popular belief to the contrary, have a voice.

WEEK 11: Animal Trivia

■ **Interjection, Colon, Hyphen (Single-Thought Adjectives), Apostrophe**

Aha heres a little known fact starfish breathe through their feet.

■ **Parallelism, Using the Right Word, End Punctuation**

Does a cricket sing with it's wings and can here with it's legs.

■ **Subject-Verb Agreement, Numbers, Spelling**

Niether my inteligent brother nor his brainy friends knows that birds

have 3 eyelids on each eye.

■ **Apostrophe (Possessives), Parentheses, Numbers**

A cats grace comes from its having 250 bones in its body twenty in its

tail alone.

■ **Numbers, Pronoun-Antecedent Agreement, Subject-Verb Agreement, Comma (Between Independent Clauses)**

Cats may have 9 lives but it has only four rows of whiskers.

WEEK 11: Corrected Sentences

- **Interjection, Colon, Hyphen (Single-Thought Adjectives), Apostrophe**

  Aha, heres a little-known fact, starfish breathe through their feet.

  Corrections: Aha! Here's ... fact: starfish

- **Parallelism, Using the Right Word, End Punctuation**

  Does a cricket sing with *its* wings and ~~can here~~ *hear* with *its* legs?

- **Subject-Verb Agreement, Numbers, Spelling**

  Neither my *intelligent* brother nor his brainy friends *know* that birds

  have *three* eyelids on each eye.

- **Apostrophe (Possessives), Parentheses, Numbers**

  A cat's grace comes from its having 250 bones in its body, *or delete word all together* (*20* ~~twenty~~ in its

  tail alone).

- **Numbers, Pronoun-Antecedent Agreement, Subject-Verb Agreement, Comma (Between Independent Clauses)**

  Cats may have *nine* lives, but *they have* only four rows of whiskers.

WEEK 12: Birds, Beasts, Insects, and Fish

■ **Double Subject, Subject-Verb Agreement, Colon or Dash, Capitalization**

the Hummingbird it have a special talent flying backward.

■ **Comma (To Separate Phrases and Clauses), Subject-Verb Agreement, Pronoun-Antecedent Agreement**

Famous for its teeth the shark have no bones in their skeleton.

■ **Comma (Dialogue), Capitalization, Quotation Marks, End Punctuation**

i asked my Biology teacher "what do camels keep in their humps

he replied they keep fat, not water."

■ **Comma (To Separate Adjectives), Hyphen (Single-Thought Adjectives), Double Negative**

New Zealand has both kiwi fruits and kiwis, which are stout long billed

birds that don't never fly.

■ **Using the Right Word, Hyphen (Single-Thought Adjectives), Parallelism, Comma (Series)**

Insects are real numerous not terribly popular and they are sometimes

mean looking.

WEEK 12: Corrected Sentences

■ **Double Subject, Subject-Verb Agreement, Colon or Dash, Capitalization**

T h   has   (or) —

~~t~~he ~~H~~ummingbird ~~it~~ ~~have~~ a special talent‸flying backward.

■ **Comma (To Separate Phrases and Clauses), Subject-Verb Agreement, Pronoun-Antecedent Agreement**

          has   its

Famous for its teeth‸the shark ~~have~~ no bones in ~~their~~ skeleton.

■ **Comma (Dialogue), Capitalization, Quotation Marks, End Punctuation**

I   b   W   ?"

~~i~~ asked my ~~B~~iology teacher‸"~~w~~hat do camels keep in their humps‸

H "T

~~h~~e replied‸~~t~~hey keep fat, not water."

■ **Comma (To Separate Adjectives), Hyphen (Single-Thought Adjectives), Double Negative**

New Zealand has both kiwi fruits and kiwis, which are stout‸long‸billed

birds that don't ~~never~~ fly.

■ **Using the Right Word, Hyphen (Single-Thought Adjectives), Parallelism, Comma (Series)**

    very

Insects are ~~real~~ numerous‸not terribly popular‸and ~~they are~~ sometimes

mean‸looking.

WEEK 13: Animal Facts

■ **Using the Right Word, Apostrophe, Hyphen, Plurals**

If iguanas wore suits, theyd need creative tailors since there body's are two thirds tail.

■ **Using the Right Word, Comma (To Separate Phrases and Clauses), Parentheses**

Although the blue whale looks as a vary large fish it is actually a humungous mammal it can reach lengths of 95 feet or more.

■ **Apostrophe (Possessives), Using the Right Word, End Punctuation, Capitalization**

did you know that the blew whales heart is about the size of a Subcompact car

■ **Interjection, Using the Right Word, Subject-Verb Agreement, End Punctuation**

Wow a butterfly taste it's food buy stepping on it

■ **Comma (To Separate Phrases and Clauses), Using the Right Word, Verb (Tense)**

Just as human fingernails rattlesnake scales were made of keratin.

WEEK 13: Corrected Sentences

■ **Using the Right Word, Apostrophe, Hyphen, Plurals**

If iguanas wore suits, they'd need creative tailors since ~~there body's~~ *their bodies* are

two-thirds tail.

■ **Using the Right Word, Comma (To Separate Phrases and Clauses), Parentheses**

Although the blue whale looks ~~as~~ *like* a ~~vary~~ *very* large fish, it is actually a

humungous mammal (it can reach lengths of 95 feet or more)

■ **Apostrophe (Possessives), Using the Right Word, End Punctuation, Capitalization**

Did you know that the ~~blew~~ *blue* whale's heart is about the size of a

subcompact car?

■ **Interjection, Using the Right Word, Subject-Verb Agreement, End Punctuation**

Wow! A butterfly ~~taste it's~~ *tastes its* food ~~buy~~ *by* stepping on it.

■ **Comma (To Separate Phrases and Clauses), Using the Right Word, Verb (Tense)**

Just ~~as~~ *like* human fingernails, rattlesnake scales ~~were~~ *are* made of keratin.

WEEK 14: Animals Great and Small

■ **Double Subject, Subject-Verb Agreement, End Punctuation**

Do you know that the smallest dinosaurs they was about the size

of chickens

■ **Comma (Numbers), Using the Right Word, Apostrophe (Possessives), Capitalization**

a Giant anteaters diet consists of up to 30000 aunts in a single day.

■ **Verb (Irregular), Using the Right Word, Run-On Sentence**

I seen the giant panda at the zoo it's related to the raccoon, not the bare.

■ **Comma (Interruptions and To Separate Phrases and Clauses), Comma Splice, Spelling, Subject-Verb Agreement**

Like birds and other animals fish build nests, Siamese fighting fish for

example builds nests of air bubles.

■ **Capitalization, Comma (Numbers), Using the Right Word**

a Bullfrog can lie 20000 eggs at once.

WEEK 14: Corrected Sentences

■ **Double Subject, Subject-Verb Agreement, End Punctuation**

Do you know that the smallest dinosaurs ~~they was~~ *were* about the size

of chickens*?*

■ **Comma (Numbers), Using the Right Word, Apostrophe (Possessives), Capitalization**

A *g*
~~a~~ *G*iant anteaters*'* diet consists of up to 30*,*000 ~~aunts~~ *ants* in a single day.

■ **Verb (Irregular), Using the Right Word, Run-On Sentence**

saw   *(or)⊙ I*   *bear*
I ~~seen~~ the giant panda at the zoo*;* it's related to the raccoon, not the ~~bare.~~

■ **Comma (Interruptions and To Separate Phrases and Clauses), Comma Splice, Spelling, Subject-Verb Agreement**

Like birds and other animals*,* fish build nests*; (or) ⊙* Siamese fighting fish*,* for
                                                                      build   *bubbles*
example*,* ~~builds~~ nests of air ~~bubles.~~

■ **Capitalization, Comma (Numbers), Using the Right Word**

A *b*   *lay*
~~a~~ *B*ullfrog can ~~lie~~ 20*,*000 eggs at once.

WEEK 15: Around the World

■ **Numbers, Abbreviations, Capitalization, Using the Right Word**

40% of the netherlands lays underwater.

■ **Numbers, Capitalization, Apostrophe (Possessives)**

90 Million People are added to the Worlds population each year.

■ **Capitalization, Using the Right Word, Semicolon**

Both the countries of guatemala and belize border mexico they are too the South.

■ **Subject-Verb Agreement, Using the Right Word, Spelling**

The Great Pyramid of Khufu in Egypt were bilt with more than too million blocks waying two tons each.

■ **Using the Right Word, End Punctuation, Quotation Marks**

Whom here new that uranium is a medal mined for use in nuclear reactors asked the teacher.

WEEK 15: Corrected Sentences

■ **Numbers, Abbreviations, Capitalization, Using the Right Word**

Forty percent   *N*   *lies*
~~40%~~ of the ~~n~~etherlands ~~lays~~ underwater.

■ **Numbers, Capitalization, Apostrophe (Possessives)**

Ninety m   *p*   *W* *'*
~~90~~ ~~M~~illion ~~P~~eople are added to the ~~W~~orld~~s~~ population each year.

■ **Capitalization, Using the Right Word, Semicolon**

                        G   *B*   *M*   *to*
Both the countries of ~~g~~uatemala and ~~b~~elize border ~~m~~exico; they are ~~too~~ the

s
~~S~~outh.

■ **Subject-Verb Agreement, Using the Right Word, Spelling**

                                         was built   *two*
The Great Pyramid of Khufu in Egypt ~~were~~ ~~bilt~~ with more than ~~too~~

               weighing
million blocks ~~waying~~ two tons each.

■ **Using the Right Word, End Punctuation, Quotation Marks**

" Who   *knew*   *metal*
~~Whom~~ here ~~new~~ that uranium is a ~~medal~~ mined for use in nuclear

       ?"
reactors asked the teacher.

WEEK 16: Geography Facts

■ **Sentence Fragment, Capitalization, Adjective (Comparative/Superlative)**

greenland, the most large island in the world, administered by denmark.

■ **Comma (Nonrestrictive Phrases and Clauses), Using the Right Word, Abbreviations**

The Petrified Forest located in the Painted Dessert of Ariz. is a hole

forest of trees turned to stone by ancient volcanic lava.

■ **Abbreviations, Numbers, Hyphen, Subject-Verb Agreement, Capitalization, Comma (Between Independent Clauses)**

1/2 of the people of nev. lives in las vegas and the other half live outside it.

■ **Comma (Appositives and Addresses), Spelling, Capitalization, Period**

mt vesuvius the only active volcano in Europe erupted and completly

buried the city of pompeii italy in C.E. 79.

■ **Apostrophe (Possessives), Adjective (Articles), Colon, Wordy Sentence**

Iraq has been the worlds leading exporter of a edible natural resource

dates, which people eat.

WEEK 16: Corrected Sentences

■ **Sentence Fragment, Capitalization, Adjective (Comparative/Superlative)**

G   *largest*   *is*   D

greenland, the ~~most large~~ island in the world, administered by denmark.

■ **Comma (Nonrestrictive Phrases and Clauses), Using the Right Word, Abbreviations**

                                    Desert   *Arizona*   *whole*

The Petrified Forest located in the Painted ~~Dessert~~ of ~~Ariz.~~ is a ~~hole~~

forest of trees turned to stone by ancient volcanic lava.

■ **Abbreviations, Numbers, Hyphen, Subject-Verb Agreement, Capitalization, Comma (Between Independent Clauses)**

One-half   *Nevada* *live*   L   V

~~1/2~~ of the people of ~~nev. lives~~ in las vegas and the other half live outside it.

■ **Comma (Appositives and Addresses), Spelling, Capitalization, Period**

M V   *completely*

mt. vesuvius, the only active volcano in Europe, erupted and ~~completly~~

                             P   I

buried the city of pompeii, italy, in C.E. 79.

■ **Apostrophe (Possessives), Adjective (Articles), Colon, Wordy Sentence**

                        '   *an*

Iraq has been the worlds leading exporter of ~~a~~ edible natural resource:

dates~~, which people eat.~~

WEEK 17: Geography from Coal to Coffee

■ **Capitalization, Numbers, Abbreviations, Comma (Series), Colon**

new york city includes the following 5 boroughs bronx brooklyn manhattan queens & staten island.

■ **Comma (To Separate Phrases and Clauses), Apostrophe, Adjective (Articles), Pronoun (Reflexive)**

If you could crush an lump of coal with enough pressure youd get a diamond for you like the ones mined in South Africa.

■ **Numbers, Abbreviations, Subject-Verb Agreement**

Only thirty % of the planet Earth were covered with ice during the last ice age.

■ **Capitalization, Using the Right Word, Abbreviations, Plurals**

brazil is the so. american country who produces the most coffees.

■ **Using the Right Word, Apostrophe (Possessives), Capitalization**

the too oceans that lap africas shores are the atlantic and the indian.

WEEK 17: Corrected Sentences

■ **Capitalization, Numbers, Abbreviations, Comma (Series), Colon**

N Y C   *five*   B   B   M

new york city includes the following 5 boroughs: bronx, brooklyn, manhattan,

Q   and S   I

queens, & staten island.

■ **Comma (To Separate Phrases and Clauses), Apostrophe, Adjective (Articles), Pronoun (Reflexive)**

                   a

If you could crush an lump of coal with enough pressure, youd get a

              yourself

diamond for you like the ones mined in South Africa.

■ **Numbers, Abbreviations, Subject-Verb Agreement**

        30 percent   *was*

Only thirty % of the planet Earth were covered with ice during the last

ice age.

■ **Capitalization, Using the Right Word, Abbreviations, Plurals**

B   South A   *that*   *coffee*

brazil is the so. american country who produces the most coffees.

■ **Using the Right Word, Apostrophe (Possessives), Capitalization**

T   *two*   A '   A   I

the too oceans that lap africas shores are the atlantic and the indian.

WEEK 18: Science Facts Great and Small

■ **Using the Right Word, Abbreviations, Verb (Irregular), Spelling, Numbers**

Some scientists believe that our sun has shined for 5 billion yrs. and will

probly continue doing sew for another 5 billion years.

■ **Comma (Between Independent Clauses), Using the Right Word**

Human eyes see things upside down but our amazing brain turns them

rite side up again.

■ **Comma (To Enclose Information and Nonrestrictive Phrases and Clauses), Using the Right Word**

Alice Watson Ph.D. learned us that tidal waves which travel as fast as

speeding bullets are caused by underwater earthquakes.

■ **Using the Right Word, Comma (To Separate Phrases and Clauses)**

Although sum people give there's a better workout then others do the

tongue is usually the strongest muscle in the human body.

■ **Subject-Verb Agreement, Comma Splice, Pronoun-Antecedent Agreement, Comma (Interruptions)**

Taste buds is not permanent bumps on your tongue, surprisingly

it survive only a few days.

WEEK 18: Corrected Sentences

■ **Using the Right Word, Abbreviations, Verb (Irregular), Spelling, Numbers**

Some scientists believe that our sun has ~~shined~~ *shone* for ~~5~~ *five* billion ~~yrs.~~ *years* and will ~~probly~~ *probably* continue doing ~~sew~~ *so* for another ~~5~~ *five* billion years.

■ **Comma (Between Independent Clauses), Using the Right Word**

Human eyes see things upside down, but our amazing brain turns them ~~rite~~ *right* side up again.

■ **Comma (To Enclose Information and Nonrestrictive Phrases and Clauses), Using the Right Word**

Alice Watson, Ph.D., ~~learned~~ *taught* us that tidal waves, which travel as fast as speeding bullets, are caused by underwater earthquakes.

■ **Using the Right Word, Comma (To Separate Phrases and Clauses)**

Although ~~sum~~ *some* people give ~~there's~~ *theirs* a better workout ~~then~~ *than* others do, the tongue is usually the strongest muscle in the human body.

■ **Subject-Verb Agreement, Comma Splice, Pronoun-Antecedent Agreement, Comma (Interruptions)**

Taste buds ~~is~~ *are* not permanent bumps on your tongue; (or) . S surprisingly, ~~it~~ *they* survive only a few days.

WEEK 19: Science Class

■ **Comma (Addresses and Nonrestrictive Phrases and Clauses), Apostrophe (Possessives), Misplaced Modifier**

From Wildrose North Dakota which is caused by the moon blocking the suns light I watched a total eclipse of the sun.

■ **Colon, Comma (Nonrestrictive Phrases and Clauses), Spelling**

Earth's core which measures aproximatly 10,000 degrees Fahrenheit is almost as hot as the surface of the source of that heat the sun.

■ **Comma (Between Independent Clauses), Subject-Verb Agreement, Apostrophe, Using the Right Word**

My science teacher say that air resistance push up against falling objects and thats why raindrops are shaped more like hamburger buns then tears.

■ **Subject-Verb Agreement, Adjective (Articles), Comma (To Separate Adjectives)**

Cinnamon come from the hard dried bark of a evergreen tree.

■ **Spelling, Comma (Interruptions), Using the Right Word**

A light-year is measured like every sceientist knows not by time, but by the distance that light travels in a year.

WEEK 19: Corrected Sentences

- **Comma (Addresses and Nonrestrictive Phrases and Clauses), Apostrophe (Possessives), Misplaced Modifier**

  From Wildrose, North Dakota, ~~which is caused by the moon blocking the suns light~~ , *which is caused by the moon blocking the sun's light* I watched a total eclipse of the sun.

- **Colon, Comma (Nonrestrictive Phrases and Clauses), Spelling**

  Earth's core, which measures *approximately* ~~aproximatly~~ 10,000 degrees Fahrenheit, is almost as hot as the surface of the source of that heat: the sun.

- **Comma (Between Independent Clauses), Subject-Verb Agreement, Apostrophe, Using the Right Word**

  My science teacher *says* ~~say~~ that air resistance *pushes* ~~push~~ up against falling objects, and that's why raindrops are shaped more like hamburger buns *than* ~~then~~ tears.

- **Subject-Verb Agreement, Adjective (Articles), Comma (To Separate Adjectives)**

  Cinnamon *comes* ~~come~~ from the hard, dried bark of *an* ~~a~~ evergreen tree.

- **Spelling, Comma (Interruptions), Using the Right Word**

  A light-year is measured, *as* ~~like~~ every *scientist* ~~sceientist~~ knows, not by time, but by the distance that light travels in a year.

WEEK 20: Science Lab

■ **Numbers, Comma (Unnecessary), Adjective (Articles), Plurals**

1,000,000 different, common-cold virus's can fit on the head, of an pin.

■ **Comma (Addresses and Unnecessary), Apostrophe (Possessives), Rambling Sentence, Numbers, Pronoun (Reflexive)**

In Padua Italy, Galileo constructed the first telescope for hiself in 1609, and discovered 4 of Jupiters moons, and he has been called the founder of modern science.

■ **Capitalization, Apostrophe (Possessives), Italics and Underlining**

Galileos published work that defended the Copernican theory was titled Dialogue concerning the two chief World Systems.

■ **Misplaced Modifier, Comma (Nonrestrictive Phrases and Clauses)**

The liver is the longest gland in the human body, which secretes important digestive enzymes.

■ **Comma (Appositives), Capitalization, Spelling**

Copernicus a polish astronomer who lived in the sixteenth sentry was the first to suggest that planets orbit the sun.

WEEK 20: Corrected Sentences

■ **Numbers, Comma (Unnecessary), Adjective (Articles), Plurals**

One million   *viruses*   *a*
~~1,000,000~~ different, common-cold ~~virus's~~ can fit on the head, of ~~an~~ pin.

■ **Comma (Addresses and Unnecessary), Apostrophe (Possessives), Rambling Sentence, Numbers, Pronoun (Reflexive)**

                                                           himself
In Padua, Italy, Galileo constructed the first telescope for ~~hiself~~ in 1609,

             four   *H*
and discovered 4 of Jupiter's moons. and he has been called the founder of

modern science.

■ **Capitalization, Apostrophe (Possessives), Italics and Underlining**

       '
Galileo's published work that defended the Copernican theory was titled

          C   *T*   *C*
<u>Dialogue concerning the two chief World Systems.</u>

■ **Misplaced Modifier, Comma (Nonrestrictive Phrases and Clauses)**

, which secretes important digestive enzymes,
    The liver is the longest gland in the human body. ~~which secretes~~

~~important digestive enzymes.~~

■ **Comma (Appositives), Capitalization, Spelling**

            P   *century*
Copernicus, a polish astronomer who lived in the sixteenth ~~sentry~~ was the

first to suggest that planets orbit the sun.

WEEK 21: The Earth and You

■ **Using the Right Word, Adverb (Comparative/Superlative), End Punctuation**

Did you know that sound travels through steal more fast than threw air.

■ **Adjective (Comparative/Superlative), Comma (Interruptions), Spelling, Apostrophe (Possessives)**

Why do you suppose is Earths gravity more weaker at the equater?

■ **Apostrophe (Possessives), Numbers, Plurals**

A persons' mouth makes 4 cup of saliva each day.

■ **Double Negative, Comma (Between Independent Clauses), Plurals, Nonstandard Language**

Many of the pollution problems on earth could of been prevented but many societys didn't know no better or didn't care.

■ **Capitalization, Using the Right Word, Comma (Series)**

Your Heart is shaped like a pare is about the size of you're fist and lays just left of center in your chest cavity.

WEEK 21: Corrected Sentences

■ **Using the Right Word, Adverb (Comparative/Superlative), End Punctuation**

Did you know that sound travels through ~~steal~~ *steel* ~~more~~ ~~fast~~ *faster* *through* than ~~threw~~ air. *?*

■ **Adjective (Comparative/Superlative), Comma (Interruptions), Spelling, Apostrophe (Possessives)**

Why, do you suppose, is Earths' gravity ~~more~~ weaker at the ~~equater~~? *equator*

■ **Apostrophe (Possessives), Numbers, Plurals**

A persons' mouth makes ~~4~~ ~~cup~~ *four cups* of saliva each day.

■ **Double Negative, Comma (Between Independent Clauses), Plurals, Nonstandard Language**

Many of the pollution problems on earth could ~~of~~ *have* been prevented, but
many ~~societys~~ *societies* didn't know ~~no~~ *any* better or didn't care.

■ **Capitalization, Using the Right Word, Comma (Series)**

Your ~~H~~*h*eart is shaped like a ~~pare~~, *pear* is about the size of ~~you're~~ *your* fist, and ~~lays~~ *lies*

just left of center in your chest cavity.

WEEK 22: Science Insights

■ **Using the Right Word, Verb (Irregular), Pronoun (Reflexive)**

A black whole is really a star that has growed so large and heavy that it has collapsed on himself.

■ **Capitalization, Italics and Underlining, Dash**

unmanned spaceships Viking I and Viking II traveled to mars in 1976.

■ **Quotation Marks, Subject-Verb Agreement, Spelling**

Both students and the black circles in the middel of your eyes is called pupils.

■ **Semicolon, Subject-Verb Agreement, Adverb (Comparative/Superlative)**

Even trees rest they grow more slow at night and pick up the pace when the sun come up.

■ **Comma (To Separate Adjectives), Adjective (Comparative/Superlative), Using the Right Word**

Wind and rain ware down even the most highest most rockiest mountains.

WEEK 22: Corrected Sentences

■ **Using the Right Word, Verb (Irregular), Pronoun (Reflexive)**

A black ~~whole~~ *hole* is really a star that has ~~growed~~ *grown* so large and heavy that it has collapsed on ~~himself~~ *itself*.

■ **Capitalization, Italics and Underlining, Dash**

~~u~~*U*nmanned spaceships_Viking I and Viking II_traveled to ~~m~~*M*ars in 1976.

■ **Quotation Marks, Subject-Verb Agreement, Spelling**

Both students and the black circles in the ~~middel~~ *middle* of your eyes ~~is~~ *are* called "pupils."

■ **Semicolon, Subject-Verb Agreement, Adverb (Comparative/Superlative)**

Even trees rest*;*they grow ~~more slow~~ *slowly* at night and pick up the pace when the sun ~~come~~ *comes* up.

■ **Comma (To Separate Adjectives), Adjective (Comparative/Superlative), Using the Right Word**

Wind and rain ~~ware~~ *wear* down even the ~~most~~ highest*,* ~~most~~ rockiest mountains.

WEEK 23: Ancient World History

■ **Using the Right Word, Wordy Sentence, Spelling**

Did you no that slaves were among the first "commodities" traded and

exchanged for other useful items in human comunities?

■ **Using the Right Word, Comma (Unnecessary and Series), Capitalization**

wrestling was vary common in Ancient Greece became a popular sport by

3000 B.C.E. and was one of the few sports, included in the first olympics.

■ **Verb (Tense), Period, Capitalization, Parentheses**

leprosy a bacterial infection was one of the first widespread human

diseases; it appears in india as early as 1500 BCE.

■ **Abbreviations, Subject-Verb Agreement, Sentence Fragment**

The 1st recorded Olympic Games. Was held in Greece in 776 B.C.E.

■ **Comma (Appositives and Dialogue), Quotation Marks, Capitalization**

herodotus the Greek historian said "The Phoenicians introduced into greece

the knowledge of letters.

WEEK 23: Corrected Sentences

■ **Using the Right Word, Wordy Sentence, Spelling**

Did you ~~no~~ *know* that slaves were among the first "commodities" traded ~~and~~ ~~exchanged for other useful items~~ in human ~~comunities~~ *communities*?

■ **Using the Right Word, Comma (Unnecessary and Series), Capitalization**

*W*restling was ~~vary~~ *very* common in *A*ncient Greece, became a popular sport by 3000 B.C.E., and was one of the few sports, included in the first *O*lympics.

■ **Verb (Tense), Period, Capitalization, Parentheses**

*L*eprosy (a bacterial infection) was one of the first widespread human diseases; it ~~appears~~ *appeared* in *I*ndia as early as 1500 B.C.E.

■ **Abbreviations, Subject-Verb Agreement, Sentence Fragment**

The ~~1st~~ *first* recorded Olympic Games, *were* ~~was~~ held in Greece in 776 B.C.E.

■ **Comma (Appositives and Dialogue), Quotation Marks, Capitalization**

*H*erodotus, the Greek historian, said, "The Phoenicians introduced into *G*reece the knowledge of letters."

WEEK 24: World History Before 1000

- **Apostrophe (Possessives), Using the Right Word, Comma (Appositives), Verb (Tense)**

  Julius Caesar is killed in 44 B.C.E. by Brutus and Cassius two of Caesars' friends who he trusted most.

- **Capitalization, Verb (Irregular), Comma (Unnecessary)**

  Attila the Hun fighted with rome, during the final years of the roman empire.

- **Colon, Italics and Underlining, Adjective (Articles)**

  Locadio's Apprentice is a book about a Italian city that experienced one of the worst volcanic disasters in history Pompeii.

- **Using the Right Word, Subject-Verb Agreement, Spelling**

  Did you no that the printing of books were diveloped in China around C.E. 600?

- **Comma Splice, Abbreviations, Comma (Series)**

  The first missile weapon was made of sulfur, rock salt, resin and petroleum in c.e. 671, it was called "Greek fire."

WEEK 24: Corrected Sentences

■ **Apostrophe (Possessives), Using the Right Word, Comma (Appositives), Verb (Tense)**

Julius Caesar ~~is~~ *was* killed in 44 B.C.E. by Brutus and Cassius,two of

Caesar's
~~Caesars'~~ friends ~~who~~ *whom* he trusted most.

■ **Capitalization, Verb (Irregular), Comma (Unnecessary)**

Attila the Hun ~~fighted~~ *fought* with *R*ome, during the final years of the *R*oman

*E*mpire.

■ **Colon, Italics and Underlining, Adjective (Articles)**

an
Locadio's Apprentice is a book about ~~a~~ Italian city that experienced one of

the worst volcanic disasters in history,Pompeii.

■ **Using the Right Word, Subject-Verb Agreement, Spelling**

know   *was developed*
Did you ~~no~~ that the printing of books ~~were~~ ~~diveloped~~ in China around

C.E. 600?

■ **Comma Splice, Abbreviations, Comma (Series)**

The first missile weapon was made of sulfur, rock salt, resin,and

CE   *(or) . I*
petroleum in ~~c.e.~~ 671,it was called "Greek fire."

WEEK 25: World History: 1000-1300

■ **Capitalization, Comma (Between Independent Clauses), Abbreviations**

the chinese invented gunpowder around c.e. 1000 but they used it for fireworks, not guns.

■ **Capitalization, Verb (Tense), Spelling**

in 1066, william the conqueror defeated england in the battle of hastings and makes french the offical language of england.

■ **Using the Right Word, Verb (Tense), Spelling**

In 1271, Marco Polo traveled to China, wear he remains fore 17 years as a state employe of Emperor Kubla Khan.

■ **Verb (Tense), Comma (Series and Appositives), Spelling**

In 1231, Pope Gregory IX began the Inquisition a campaign to find bring to trial and punish people who hold controversial beleifs.

■ **Subject-Verb Agreement, Adjective (Articles), Capitalization, Colon or Dash**

The famous oxford university were founded in 1167 by an jewish scholar ibn ezra.

WEEK 25: Corrected Sentences

■ **Capitalization, Comma (Between Independent Clauses), Abbreviations**

T   C   CE
The Chinese invented gunpowder around c.e. 1000, but they used it for

fireworks, not guns.

■ **Capitalization, Verb (Tense), Spelling**

I   W   C   E   B   H
In 1066, William the Conqueror defeated England in the battle of Hastings

            made F   official   E
and ~~makes~~ french the ~~offical~~ language of england.

■ **Using the Right Word, Verb (Tense), Spelling**

                                                    where   remained for
In 1271, Marco Polo traveled to China, ~~wear~~ he ~~remains fore~~ 17 years as

                employee
a state ~~employe~~ of Emperor Kubla Khan.

■ **Verb (Tense), Comma (Series and Appositives), Spelling**

In 1231, Pope Gregory IX began the Inquisition, a campaign to find, bring

                                    held   beliefs
to trial, and punish people who ~~hold~~ controversial ~~beleifs~~.

■ **Subject-Verb Agreement, Adjective (Articles), Capitalization, Colon or Dash**

                O   U   was   a J   (or) —
The famous Oxford University ~~were~~ founded in 1167 by ~~an~~ jewish scholar :

I   E
Ibn ezra.

WEEK 26: World History: The Middle Ages

■ **Comma (Appositives and Interruptions), Apostrophe (Possessives)**

The bubonic plague also known as the Black Death first appeared in Europe in 1347; by 1350 it had killed incredibly almost half of Europes populace.

■ **Numbers, Using the Right Word, Capitalization**

joan of arc was only 17 when she lead battles against the english in the 1420s and only nineteen when she was burned at the stake.

■ **Comma (To Separate Phrases and Clauses), Colon or Dash, Apostrophe**

Because the Catholic church wouldnt grant him a divorce Henry VIII established his own church in 1533; the Protestant Church of England.

■ **Comma (Appositives), Apostrophe (Possessives), Capitalization, Dash**

elizabeth I henrys VIIIs daughter had one of the longest reigns 45 years in english history.

■ **Comma (To Separate Phrases and Clauses and To Separate Adjectives), Using the Right Word, Wordy Sentence**

In the sixteenth and seventeenth centuries Puritans were deported from England and asked to leave for there strict unpopular religious beliefs.

WEEK 26: Corrected Sentences

■ **Comma (Appositives and Interruptions), Apostrophe (Possessives)**

The bubonic plague, also known as the Black Death, first appeared in Europe

in 1347; by 1350 it had killed, incredibly, almost half of Europe's populace.

■ **Numbers, Using the Right Word, Capitalization**

Joan of Arc was only 17 when she led battles against the English in the

1420s and only nineteen (19) when she was burned at the stake.

■ **Comma (To Separate Phrases and Clauses), Colon or Dash, Apostrophe**

Because the Catholic church wouldn't grant him a divorce, Henry VIII

established his own church in 1533: (or) — the Protestant Church of England.

■ **Comma (Appositives), Apostrophe (Possessives), Capitalization, Dash**

Elizabeth I, Henry VIII's daughter, had one of the longest reigns — 45 years —

in English history.

■ **Comma (To Separate Phrases and Clauses and To Separate Adjectives), Using the Right Word, Wordy Sentence**

In the sixteenth and seventeenth centuries, Puritans were deported from

England and asked to leave for their strict, unpopular religious beliefs.

WEEK 27: World History: The Last Two Centuries

■ **Capitalization, Apostrophe, Quotation Marks, Pronoun (Reflexive)**

its been said "that napoleon crowned Napoleon emperor of france in 1804."

■ **Capitalization, Verb (Tense), Wordy Sentence, Spelling**

england abolishes slavry in 1807 and simply gave up the practice of

holding slaves.

■ **Comma (Appositives and Nonrestrictive Phrases and Clauses), Capitalization, Using the Right Word**

in 1839, and again in 1856 england waged war against china in order too

win the rite to sell opium a drug to the chinese people.

■ **Comma (Dates), Numbers, Abbreviations, Capitalization, Parentheses**

the russian revolution began in March, 1917 and ended 3 yrs. later when

the Union of soviet socialist Republics U.S.S.R. was established.

■ **Using the Right Word, Adjective (Articles), Numbers**

A estimated 60,000,000 people dyed during World War II.

WEEK 27: Corrected Sentences

■ **Capitalization, Apostrophe, Quotation Marks, Pronoun (Reflexive)**

I've "that Napoleon crowned ~~Napoleon~~ *himself* emperor of France in 1804."

■ **Capitalization, Verb (Tense), Wordy Sentence, Spelling**

England ~~abolishes slavry~~ *abolished slavery* in 1807. ~~and simply gave up the practice of holding slaves.~~

■ **Comma (Appositives and Nonrestrictive Phrases and Clauses), Capitalization, Using the Right Word**

In 1839, and again in 1856, England waged war against China in order ~~too~~ *to* win the ~~rite~~ *right* to sell opium, a drug, to the Chinese people.

■ **Comma (Dates), Numbers, Abbreviations, Capitalization, Parentheses**

The Russian Revolution began in March, 1917 and ended ~~3 yrs.~~ *three years* later when the Union of Soviet Socialist Republics (U.S.S.R.) was established.

■ **Using the Right Word, Adjective (Articles), Numbers**

~~A~~ *An* estimated ~~60,000,000~~ *60 million* people ~~dyed~~ *died* during World War II.

WEEK 28: Wise Sayings

■ **Comma (To Separate Phrases and Clauses), Subject-Verb Agreement**

The mind like a parachute function only when open.

■ **Subject-Verb Agreement, Capitalization, Comma (Unnecessary), Parallelism**

To enjoy Freedom we, has to be controlling ourselves.

—Virginia Woolf

■ **Comma (To Separate Adjectives), Adjective (Comparative/Superlative)**

Freedom is the last better hope of earth.

—Abraham Lincoln

■ **Comma (To Separate Phrases and Clauses), Using the Right Word, Spelling**

When people are free to do like they pleese they usually imitate each other.

—Eric Hoffer

■ **Comma (Between Independent Clauses), Double Negative, Spelling**

Thousands of candles can be lighted from a single candle and the life of the candle will not never be shortened; happyness never decreases by being shared.

—Buddha

WEEK 28: Corrected Sentences

■ **Comma (To Separate Phrases and Clauses), Subject-Verb Agreement**

functions
The mind, like a parachute, ~~function~~ only when open.

■ **Subject-Verb Agreement, Capitalization, Comma (Unnecessary), Parallelism**

f   *have*   *control*
To enjoy Freedom we, ~~has~~ to ~~be controlling~~ ourselves.

—Virginia Woolf

■ **Comma (To Separate Adjectives), Adjective (Comparative/Superlative)**

best
Freedom is the last, ~~better~~ hope of earth.

—Abraham Lincoln

■ **Comma (To Separate Phrases and Clauses), Using the Right Word, Spelling**

as   *please*
When people are free to do ~~like~~ they ~~pleese~~, they usually imitate each other.

—Eric Hoffer

■ **Comma (Between Independent Clauses), Double Negative, Spelling**

Thousands of candles can be lighted from a single candle, and the life

happiness
of the candle will not ~~never~~ be shortened; ~~happyness~~ never decreases

by being shared.

—Buddha

WEEK 29: Proverbs

■ **Subject-Verb Agreement, Double Negative**

Joys does not never stay but take wing and fly away.

—Martial

■ **Pronoun-Antecedent Agreement, Subject-Verb Agreement, Using the Right Word**

Life is as a sandwich: the more you adds to it, the better they become.

■ **Quotation Marks, Comma (Dialogue), Run-On Sentence**

We don't have a goose on our farm my mother always says Don't kill the goose that laid the golden egg.

■ **Subject-Verb Agreement, Numbers, Spelling**

1 loyal friend are worth ten thousand relitives.

■ **Using the Right Word, Subject-Verb Agreement, Spelling**

Life is partly what we makes it, and partly what is maid by the freinds who we choose.

—Chinese Proverb

WEEK 29: Corrected Sentences

■ **Subject-Verb Agreement, Double Negative**

do
Joys ~~does~~ not ~~never~~ stay but take wing and fly away.

—Martial
Joy *takes* *flies*
(or) ~~Joys~~ does not ~~never~~ stay but ~~take~~ wing and ~~fly~~ away.

■ **Pronoun-Antecedent Agreement, Subject-Verb Agreement, Using the Right Word**

like *add* *it becomes*
Life is ~~as~~ a sandwich: the more you ~~adds~~ to it, the better ~~they~~ ~~become~~.

■ **Quotation Marks, Comma (Dialogue), Run-On Sentence**

but "
We don't have a goose on our farm, my mother always says, Don't kill the

"
goose that laid the golden egg.

■ **Subject-Verb Agreement, Numbers, Spelling**

One *is* *10,000* *relatives*
~~1~~ loyal friend ~~are~~ worth ~~ten thousand~~ ~~relitives~~.

■ **Using the Right Word, Subject-Verb Agreement, Spelling**

make *made* *friends*
Life is partly what we ~~makes~~ it, and partly what is ~~maid~~ by the ~~freinds~~

whom
~~who~~ we choose.

—Chinese Proverb

WEEK 30: More Proverbs

■ **Comma (Unnecessary), Using the Right Word, Verb (Tense)**

Hopes are but the dreams, of those, whom were awake.

—Pindar

■ **Apostrophe, Subject-Verb Agreement, Quotation Marks**

Success come in cans, not in "can'ts."

■ **Using the Right Word, Adjective (Comparative/Superlative)**

The pen is mightiest then the sword.

■ **Pronoun-Antecedent Agreement, Spelling, Adverb (Comparative/Superlative)**

When fools hold their tonges, he will oftener pass for wise people.

■ **Using the Right Word, Apostrophe (Possessives), Adjective (Articles)**

Gratefulness is an pour persons payment.

WEEK 30: Corrected Sentences

■ **Comma (Unnecessary), Using the Right Word, Verb (Tense)**

Hopes are but the dreams~~,~~ of those~~,~~ *who* ~~whom~~ *are* ~~were~~ awake.

—Pindar

■ **Apostrophe, Subject-Verb Agreement, Quotation Marks**

comes
Success ~~come~~ in cans, not in "can'ts."

■ **Using the Right Word, Adjective (Comparative/Superlative)**

mightier than
The pen is ~~mightiest~~ ~~then~~ the sword.

■ **Pronoun-Antecedent Agreement, Spelling, Adverb (Comparative/Superlative)**

tongues *they* *more often*
When fools hold their ~~tonges~~, ~~he~~ will ~~oftener~~ pass for wise people.

■ **Using the Right Word, Apostrophe (Possessives), Adjective (Articles)**

a poor
Gratefulness is ~~an~~ ~~pour~~ persons payment.

WEEK 31: The Environment and You

■ **Using the Right Word, Hyphen (Single-Thought Adjectives), Numbers**

Lung damage from ozone polluted air effects 3 out of 5 Americans.

■ **Double Negative, Rambling Sentence**

Americans throw away 240 to 260 million tires each year, and tires are not never biodegradable and they cause air pollution when they are burned and they are a breeding place for disease-carrying mosquitoes when they are stored outdoors.

■ **Abbreviations, Subject-Verb Agreement, Numbers**

Americans consumes 450,000,000,000 gallons of H_2O every day.

■ **Dash, Using the Right Word, Plurals, Subject-Verb Agreement**

Junk male two million tons of it stuff our mailbox's each year.

■ **Numbers, Abbreviations, Using the Right Word, Apostrophe (Possessives)**

20% of the earths species could be extinct buy the year two thousand ten.

WEEK 31: Corrected Sentences

■ **Using the Right Word, Hyphen (Single-Thought Adjectives), Numbers**

affects *three* *five*
Lung damage from ozone-polluted air ~~effects~~ ~~3~~ out of ~~5~~ Americans.

■ **Double Negative, Rambling Sentence**

Americans throw away 240 to 260 million tires each year, and tires are

not ~~never~~ biodegradable. ~~and~~ they cause air pollution when they are

burned. ~~and~~ they are a breeding place for discase-carrying mosquitoes

when they are stored outdoors.

■ **Abbreviations, Subject-Verb Agreement, Numbers**

consume *450 billion* *water*
Americans ~~consumes~~ ~~450,000,000,000~~ gallons of ~~H₂0~~ every day.

■ **Dash, Using the Right Word, Plurals, Subject-Verb Agreement**

mail— *—stuffs* *mailboxes*
Junk ~~male~~ two million tons of it ~~stuff~~ our ~~mailbox's~~ each year.

■ **Numbers, Abbreviations, Using the Right Word, Apostrophe (Possessives)**

Twenty percent *'* *by* *2010*
~~20%~~ of the earths species could be extinct ~~buy~~ the year ~~two thousand ten~~.

WEEK 32: Pollution Solution

■ **Using the Right Word, Capitalization, Abbreviations**

about half the paper used in the u.s. is four packaging.

■ **Subject-Verb Agreement, Wordy Sentence, Spelling, End Punctuation**

A running faucet send three to five gallons of precius water down the

drain every minute, allowing the water to escape

■ **Comma (To Separate Adjectives and Unnecessary), Adverb (Comparative/Superlative)**

Recycling waste solids, to turn garbage into new useful materials, is most

easily done than creating things from scratch.

■ **Colon, Comma (Series), Spelling**

The kinds of enviromental pollution include the following; water air and

soil pollution, plus that caused by solid wastes noise and radiation.

■ **Pronoun-Antecedent Agreement, Capitalization, Verb (Tense)**

since ancient times, Human Beings had polluted its environment by

dumping wastes in water and by burning fuel.

WEEK 32: Corrected Sentences

■ Using the Right Word, Capitalization, Abbreviations

A   *United States*   *for*
~~a~~bout half the paper used in the ~~u.s.~~ is ~~four~~ packaging.

■ Subject-Verb Agreement, Wordy Sentence, Spelling, End Punctuation

           sends   *precious*

A running faucet ~~send~~ three to five gallons of ~~precius~~ water down the

drain every minute. ~~allowing the water to escape~~

■ Comma (To Separate Adjectives and Unnecessary), Adverb (Comparative/Superlative)

                                                            more
Recycling waste solids, to turn garbage into new, useful materials, is ~~most~~

easily done than creating things from scratch.

■ Colon, Comma (Series), Spelling

            environmental
The kinds of ~~enviromental~~ pollution include the following: water, air, and

soil pollution, plus that caused by solid wastes, noise, and radiation.

■ Pronoun-Antecedent Agreement, Capitalization, Verb (Tense)

S   *h*   *b*   *have*   *their*
~~S~~ince ancient times, ~~H~~uman ~~B~~eings ~~had~~ polluted ~~its~~ environment by

dumping wastes in water and by burning fuel.

WEEK 33: Environmental Problems

- **Plurals, Verb (Tense), Comma (Unnecessary)**

  In the 1930s, motorists in some Midwest citys have to use headlights during the day, to see through the smog.

- **Using the Right Word, Comma (To Separate Phrases and Clauses), Numbers**

  By using leaded gasoline car owners dumped as much as two-hundred-twenty-five-thousand tons of led into the air each year.

- **Abbreviations, Comma Splice, Comma (To Separate Adjectives), Numbers**

  At least 3% of the earth's water is fresh drinkable water, however, 99.5% of that is frozen.

- **Comma (Interjections), Using the Right Word, Parentheses**

  Yes disposable diapers will lay around in landfills for five centuries 500 years before rotting away.

- **Subject-Verb Agreement, Comma (Series), Capitalization**

  increased temperatures permits insects rodents and other pests from the south to immigrate to farming regions in the north.

WEEK 33: Corrected Sentences

■ **Plurals, Verb (Tense), Comma (Unnecessary)**

In the 1930s, motorists in some Midwest ~~citys~~ ~~have~~ *cities had* to use headlights during the day*,* to see through the smog.

■ **Using the Right Word, Comma (To Separate Phrases and Clauses), Numbers**

By using leaded gasoline*,* car owners dumped as much as ~~two-hundred-twenty-five-thousand~~ *225,000* tons of ~~led~~ *lead* into the air each year.

■ **Abbreviations, Comma Splice, Comma (To Separate Adjectives), Numbers**

At least ~~3%~~ *three percent* of the earth's water is fresh*,* drinkable water*;* however, 99.5~~%~~ *percent* of that is frozen.

■ **Comma (Interjections), Using the Right Word, Parentheses**

Yes*,* disposable diapers will ~~lay~~ *lie* around in landfills for five centuries *(*500 years*)* before rotting away.

■ **Subject-Verb Agreement, Comma (Series), Capitalization**

*I*ncreased temperatures ~~permits~~ *permit* insects*,* rodents*,* and other pests from the *S*outh to immigrate to farming regions in the *N*orth.

WEEK 34: Be a Good Sport!

■ **Capitalization, Adjective (Comparative/Superlative), Combining Sentences, Numbers**

martina navratilova holds the record for the more wimbledon tennis championships. she holds the record for winning 9 titles.

■ **Comma (Addresses and To Separate Phrases and Clauses), Using the Right Word**

Although Jesse Owens won four gold metals in the 1936 Olympics in Berlin Germany Hitler refused to shake his hand because Owens was black.

■ **Capitalization, Apostrophe (Possessives), End Punctuation, Spelling**

did you know that indianapolis 500 winners traditionly drink milk in the winners circle

■ **Colon, Apostrophe, Sentence Fragment, Adjective (Articles)**

For the world championship in fencing. Youd find men and women equipped with the following a epee, a foil, or a saber.

■ **Capitalization, Comma (Direct Address), End Punctuation**

Jean did you know that sumo wrestling is the National sport of Japan.

WEEK 34: Corrected Sentences

■ **Capitalization, Adjective (Comparative/Superlative), Combining Sentences, Numbers**

M *N*
martina navratilova holds the record for the ~~more~~ *most* Wimbledon tennis

championships, ~~she holds the record for~~ winning *nine* ~~9~~ titles.

■ **Comma (Addresses and To Separate Phrases and Clauses), Using the Right Word**

Although Jesse Owens won four gold *medals* ~~metals~~ in the 1936 Olympics in Berlin,

Germany, Hitler refused to shake his hand because Owens was black.

■ **Capitalization, Apostrophe (Possessives), End Punctuation, Spelling**

D *I*
did you know that indianapolis 500 winners *traditionally* ~~traditionly~~ drink milk in the

winner's circle?

■ **Colon, Apostrophe, Sentence Fragment, Adjective (Articles)**

For the world championship in fencing, you'd find men and women

equipped with the following: *an* a epee, a foil, or a saber.

■ **Capitalization, Comma (Direct Address), End Punctuation**

Jean, did you know that sumo wrestling is the *N*ational sport of Japan?

WEEK 35: Sports Stats

■ **Capitalization, Numbers, Comma (To Separate Phrases and Clauses)**

when hank aaron retired from baseball he had seven hundred fifty-five home runs to his credit.

■ **Comma (Unnecessary), Adjective (Articles), Subject-Verb Agreement**

A catcher squat a average, of 300 times, during a baseball doubleheader.

■ **Capitalization, Subject-Verb Agreement, Comma Splice, Spelling**

the first woman to race in the indianapolis 500 were janet guthrie in 1977, she won nineth place in the race in 1978.

■ **Using the Right Word, Comma (Direct Address and Interjections), Numbers, Abbreviations**

Hey Steve did you no that Roger Bannister was the first man to run the mile in less then 4 min?

■ **Numbers, Subject-Verb Agreement, Capitalization**

14 of the 15 jockeys in the first kentucky derby was African American.

WEEK 35: Corrected Sentences

■ **Capitalization, Numbers, Comma (To Separate Phrases and Clauses)**

W   H   A   *755*

When ~~h~~ank ~~a~~aron retired from baseball,he had ~~seven hundred fifty-five~~

home runs to his credit.

■ **Comma (Unnecessary), Adjective (Articles), Subject-Verb Agreement**

           squats an

A catcher ~~squat a~~ average, of 300 times, during a baseball doubleheader.

■ **Capitalization, Subject-Verb Agreement, Comma Splice, Spelling**

T   I   *was* J   G

The first woman to race in the ~~i~~ndianapolis 500 ~~were~~ ~~j~~anet ~~g~~uthrie in

        (or)⊙ S ninth

1977, she won ~~nineth~~ place in the race in 1978.

■ **Using the Right Word, Comma (Direct Address and Interjections), Numbers, Abbreviations**

            know

Hey,Steve,did you ~~no~~ that Roger Bannister was the first man to run the

         than four minutes

mile in less ~~then 4 min~~?

■ **Numbers, Subject-Verb Agreement, Capitalization**

Fourteen fifteen   K   D   *were*

~~14~~ of the ~~15~~ jockeys in the first ~~k~~entucky ~~d~~erby ~~was~~ African American.

MUG Shot Paragraphs

The MUG Shot paragraphs are a quick and efficient way to review **m**echanics, **u**sage, and **g**rammar errors each week. These paragraphs can also serve as excellent proofreading exercises. Each paragraph can be corrected and discussed in 8 to 10 minutes.

Implementation and Evaluation   **77**

MUG Shot Paragraphs   **78**

Implementation and Evaluation

For each set of MUG Shot sentences, there is a corresponding MUG Shot paragraph. The paragraph reviews many of the editing skills covered during the week.

Implementation

A MUG Shot paragraph can be implemented at the end of the week as a review or an evaluation activity. Simply distribute copies of the week's paragraph, and have students make their corrections on the sheet. Students may use the "Editing and Proofreading Marks" in their handbooks or on page iv to use as a guide in correcting the MUG Shot paragraph. We suggest that students then discuss their changes (in pairs or in small groups). Afterward, go over the paragraph as a class to make sure that everyone understands the reasons for the changes. (You may want to refer to the corresponding MUG Shot sentences during your discussion.)

An Alternative Approach: Distribute copies of the MUG Shot paragraph along with the edited version. (They appear on the same page in your booklet.) Have students fold the edited version under, and then make their changes. Once they are finished, they can unfold the paper and check their own work.

Evaluation

If you use the paragraphs as an evaluation activity, we recommend that you give students a basic performance score for their work. This score should reflect the number of changes the student has marked correctly (before or after any discussion). The weekly score might also reflect the student's work on corresponding MUG Shot sentences.

WEEK 1: Soda Pop

■ **Using the Right Word, Comma (Interjections), Sentence Fragment, End Punctuation, Capitalization**

People in the world drink more than 260 million glasses of cola every day Wow that's nearly as many Sodas as there are people in the United States and nearly three times the number of miles from the earth to the son! People drink more Sodas than there are cubic yards of concrete in the Grand Coulee Dam. More Sodas than anyone cares to count! Why wood health-conscious people put so much fizz into there stomachs

Corrected Paragraph

People in the world drink more than 260 million glasses of cola
every day. Wow, that's nearly as many sodas as there are people in the
United States and nearly three times the number of miles from the earth
sun
to the son! People drink more sodas than there are cubic yards of
That's m   s
concrete in the Grand Coulee Dam. More sodas than anyone cares to
would   their
count! Why wood health-conscious people put so much fizz into there
?
stomachs

WEEK 2: Against All Odds

■ Comma (To Separate Phrases and Clauses), Verb (Tense and Irregular), Adjective (Comparative/Superlative), Double Subject, Hyphen

When meeting obstacles in your life remember the lives of Mozart and Beethoven. Although both of these men was great composers each one has his own obstacles to overcome. Mozart begins writing symphonies when he was a five year old and spends all of his adult life trying to overcome poverty. Beethoven he writed many of his most fine symphonies after going deaf. The drive to create can overcame many obstacles.

Corrected Paragraph

When meeting obstacles in your life,$_\wedge$ remember the lives of Mozart
                                                          were
and Beethoven. Although both of these men ~~was~~ great composers,$_\wedge$ each
   had   *began*
one ~~has~~ his own obstacles to overcome. Mozart ~~begins~~ writing symphonies
                            spent
when he was a five-year-old and ~~spends~~ all of his adult life trying to
                    wrote   *finest*
overcome poverty. Beethoven ~~he writed~~ many of his ~~most fine~~ symphonies
                                        overcome
after going deaf. The drive to create can ~~overcame~~ many obstacles.

WEEK 3: On a More Cheerful Note . . .

■ **Using the Right Word, Comma (Addresses), Apostrophe (Possessives), Spelling, Hyphen (Single-Thought Adjectives), Period**

When my West Coast ant got sick last month, my mom said I should write to her. At first it was hard to no what to say, but soon the words started too sound like me. I signed my aunts letter "Your niece, Micaela," and than I carefully addressed the envelope: Mrs Juanita Ramirez, c/o Grandview Hospital 230 Pleasant Lane, Oceanview California 90402. I hope she apreciates the self addressed, stamped envelope I enclosed. If she writes, it means she is feeling good.

Corrected Paragraph

When my West Coast ~~ant~~ *aunt* got sick last month, my mom said I should write to her. At first it was hard to ~~no~~ *know* what to say, but soon the words started ~~too~~ *to* sound like me. I signed my aunt's letter "Your niece, Micaela," and ~~than~~ *then* I carefully addressed the envelope: Mrs. Juanita Ramirez, c/o Grandview Hospital, 230 Pleasant Lane, Oceanview, California 90402. I hope she ~~apreciates~~ *appreciates* the self-addressed, stamped envelope I enclosed. If she writes, it means she is feeling ~~good~~ *well*.

WEEK 4: Old Gold Fred

■ **Using the Right Word, Wordy Sentence, Apostrophe, End Punctuation, Subject-Verb Agreement, Abbreviations**

Goldfish kept in homes usually don't lives five years. Considering that he lived to be 41 years old, Fred is the oldest goldfish on record. Mr. Wilson, Fred's owner, must have made a special point of taking care of his fishbowl pet and giving it lots of attention. He changed Fred's water and cleaned Fred's fishbowl regularly. I wonder if Mister Wilson talked too Fred, to. Dont you wonder what Fred ate

Corrected Paragraph

Goldfish kept in homes usually don't ~~lives~~ *live* five years. Considering that he lived to be 41 years old, Fred is the oldest goldfish on record. Mr. Wilson, Fred's owner, must have made a special point of taking care of his fishbowl pe~~t. and giving it lots of attention~~. He changed Fred's water and cleaned Fred's fishbowl regularly. I wonder if ~~Mister~~ *Mr.* Wilson talked ~~too~~ *to* Fred, ~~to.~~ *too*. Dont you wonder what Fred ate*?*

WEEK 5: We Protest!

■ **Using the Right Word, Comma (To Separate Phrases and Clauses), Capitalization, Misplaced Modifier, Verb (Irregular)**

To protest unfair taxes American revolutionaries through three shiploads of tea into boston harbor disguised as Indians in 1773. In an attempt to control the angry colonists, the british government past what became knowed as the "Intolerable Acts." This only served to unify the colonists too work harder for independence. The first continental congress, a gathering of representatives from 12 of the American Colonies, met as a result of the "Intolerable Acts."

Corrected Paragraph

To protest unfair taxes, American revolutionaries ~~through~~ three [disguised as Indians] [threw]
shiploads of tea into ßoston ħarbor ~~disguised as Indians~~ in 1773. In an
attempt to control the angry colonists, the ßritish government ~~past~~ what [passed]
became ~~knowed~~ as the "Intolerable Acts." This only served to unify the [known]
colonists ~~too~~ work harder for independence. The first ¢ontinental ¢ongress, [to]
a gathering of representatives from 12 of the American ¢olonies, met as a
result of the "Intolerable Acts."

WEEK 6: The Lessons of War

■ **Comma Splice, Plurals, Using the Right Word, Verb (Irregular and Tense), Capitalization**

The Mexican-american War ended in 1848, the United States gains 525,000 square miles of territory from Mexico. The United States had growed by one-fourth, Mexico had shrinked by one-half. The Mexican-American War teached many soldiers how too fight and many officers how to led. In one of his reports, captain Robert E. Lee talked in glowing terms of a young officer named Grant. Thirteen years later, these two mans would be enemys, fighting on opposite sides in the American civil war.

Corrected Paragraph

              A   )(or) ⊙ T   gained

The Mexican-american War ended in 1848, the United States gains

525,000 square miles of territory from Mexico. The United States had

  grown   )(or) ⊙   shrunk

growed by one-fourth, Mexico had shrinked by one-half. The Mexican-

       taught'   to

American War teached many soldiers how too fight and many officers how

  lead   C

to led. In one of his reports, captain Robert E. Lee talked in glowing

terms of a young officer named Grant. Thirteen years later, these two

  men   enemies   C

mans would be enemys, fighting on opposite sides in the American civil

W
war.

WEEK 7: Casualties of War

■ **Using the Right Word, Capitalization, Quotation Marks, Verb (Irregular), Comma (Interruptions)**

My History teacher said, in the Civil War, many soldiers who lived threw the battles dyed later of there wounds. He said that at the Battle of Sharpsburg near antietam creek in Maryland, more than 5,000 soldiers were slayed between sunrise and sunset. It was the bloodiest battle of the Civil War, leaving an additional 19,000 men wounded. Three thousand of these died latter of their wounds. Medical science had not unfortunately progressed to the point where it could save many of the wounded.

Corrected Paragraph

My ʰHistory teacher said, ⁶⁶Iin the Civil War, many soldiers who lived
through
~~threw~~ the battles ~~dyed~~ **died** later of ~~there~~ **their** wounds.⁹⁹ He said that at the Battle
                                                              A   C
of Sharpsburg near ántietam ¢reek in Maryland, more than 5,000 soldiers
          slain
were ~~slayed~~ between sunrise and sunset. It was the bloodiest battle of

the Civil War, leaving an additional 19,000 men wounded. Three thousand
                    later
of these died ~~latter~~ of their wounds. Medical science had not‚unfortunately‚

progressed to the point where it could save many of the wounded.

WEEK 8: A Vote for Equality

■ **Capitalization, Comma (Series, Dates, and To Separate Phrases and Clauses), Apostrophe (Possessives), Plurals, Comma Splice**

Prior to August 26 1920, woman did not have the right to vote. More than one-half the countrys adults had been kept from having any say in political affairs. With the passage of the 19th Amendment, women, as well as men, could elect Governors Senators Presidents or any other public officials. With the right to vote woman enjoyed more equality. The womens movement did not stop when women got the right to vote, that was only the beginning.

Corrected Paragraph

Prior to August 26, 1920, ~~woman~~ *women* did not have the right to vote. More than one-half the country's adults had been kept from having any say in political affairs. With the passage of the 19th Amendment, women, as well as men, could elect *g*overnors, *s*enators, *p*residents, or any other public officials. With the right to vote, ~~woman~~ *women* enjoyed more equality. The women's movement did not stop when women got the right to vote. That was only the beginning.

WEEK 9: Presidential Trivia

■ **Verb (Irregular), Adjective (Comparative/Superlative), Quotation Marks, Comma (Unnecessary), End Punctuation, Pronoun-Antecedent Agreement**

Do you know which president was the older to be swore into office? Do you know which one wore a toupee, or which one owned the most strange pet Do you know, which one raised peanuts, which one was a former movie star, or which one started their day by saying, Good morning, Lady Bird It's fun to collect trivia about a subject. You're sure to discover some interesting, and peculiar facts

Corrected Paragraph

Do you know which president was the ~~older~~ *oldest* to be ~~swore~~ *sworn* into office? Do you know which one wore a toupee/ or which one owned the ~~most~~ ~~strange~~ *strangest* pet⋅Do you know/ which one raised peanuts, which one was a former movie star, or which one started ~~their~~ *his* day by saying,"Good morning, Lady Bird"/It's fun to collect trivia about a subject. You're sure to discover some interesting/ and peculiar facts⨀

WEEK 10: Tongue-Twisted

■ **Using the Right Word, Comma (Series and Interruptions), Comma Splice, Subject-Verb Agreement, Hyphen (Single-Thought Adjectives)**

A tongue are a movable muscle attached to the floor of the mouth. Animals use their tongues to smell to maneuver and to swallow their food. Yes I find tongues interesting. There is long tongues fat tongues skinny tongues green tongues and lizard like, forked tongues, tongues are just plane fun! (Just don't stick you're tongue to a cold, medal surface, or you'll have a "thore" one!)

Corrected Paragraph

A tongue ~~are~~ *is* a movable muscle attached to the floor of the mouth. Animals use their tongues to smell, to maneuver, and to swallow their food. Yes, I find tongues interesting. There ~~is~~ *are* long tongues, fat tongues, skinny tongues, green tongues, and lizard-like, forked tongues, tongues are just ~~plane~~ *plain* fun! (Just don't stick ~~you're~~ *your* tongue to a cold, ~~medal~~ *metal* surface, or you'll have a "thore" one!)

WEEK 11: Tricky Trivia

■ **Subject-Verb Agreement, Pronoun-Antecedent Agreement, Interjection, End Punctuation, Apostrophe (Possessives), Colon**

Here are some little-known facts starfish breathe through their feet, grasshoppers antennae serves as noses, snakes smell through his tongues, a gathering of ducks are called a "brace," a female swan is known as a "pen," and scuba divers breathes through their regulators. Aha. Bet you weren't expecting that last one

Corrected Paragraph

Here are some little-known facts ∧: starfish breathe through their feet, grasshoppers' antennae ~~serves~~ *serve* as noses, snakes smell through ~~his~~ *their* tongues, a gathering of ducks ~~are~~ *is* called a "brace," a female swan is known as a "pen," and scuba divers ~~breathes~~ *breathe* through their regulators. Aha ~~.~~ **!** Bet you weren't expecting that last one ∧ **!**

WEEK 12: Seashore Treasures

■ **Comma (Series and Dialogue), Subject-Verb Agreement, Quotation Marks, Double Negative, Hyphen (Single-Thought Adjectives)**

Some people just picks up seashells from ocean beaches, but not me. I also collect pieces of sponge bits of green colored glass smoothed by the waves and sand and fossilized shark teeth. These treasures decorates shelves bookcases and the desktop in my beach theme bedroom. I even have a bell shaped, clear-glass lamp filled with shells. I said to my mom I love all my stuff. I don't want no ordinary collection.

Corrected Paragraph

Some people just ~~picks~~ *pick* up seashells from ocean beaches, but not me. I also collect pieces of sponge, bits of green-colored glass smoothed by the waves and sand, and fossilized shark teeth. These treasures ~~decorates~~ *decorate* shelves, bookcases, and the desktop in my beach-theme bedroom. I even have a bell-shaped, clear-glass lamp filled with shells. I said to my mom, "I love all my stuff. I don't want ~~no~~ *any* ordinary collection."

WEEK 13: Whale Tale

■ **Subject-Verb Agreement, Comma (To Separate Phrases and Clauses), Plurals, Parentheses, Verb (Tense)**

During the sixteenth and seventeenth centurys whale hunters obtain these valuable things from whales: baleen, used to make fishing rods and umbrellas; oil, used in lamp and candle; and "ambergris," used as a base for expensive perfumes. Because it's a huge, slow-moving target measuring up to 30 meters long the blue whale were overhunted by whaling crews. The irony is that now this whale are dependent on well-meaning humans to saves it from extinction. Will it find room in its giant heart the size of a subcompact car to trust us?

Corrected Paragraph

During the sixteenth and seventeenth ~~centurys~~ *centuries*~~,~~whale hunters ~~obtain~~ *obtained* these valuable things from whales: baleen, used to make fishing rods and umbrellas; oil, used in ~~lamp~~ *lamps* and ~~candle~~ *candles*; and "ambergris," used as a base for expensive perfumes. Because it's a huge, slow-moving target measuring up to 30 meters long*,* the blue whale ~~were~~ *was* overhunted by whaling crews. The irony is that now this whale ~~are~~ *is* dependent on well-meaning humans to ~~saves~~ *save* it from extinction. Will it find room in its giant heart*(*the size of a subcompact car*)*to trust us?

WEEK 14: Lots of Little Things

■ **Subject-Verb Agreement, Double Subject, Run-On Sentence, Comma Splice, Comma (Numbers), Verb (Irregular)**

A bullfrog can lay 20000 eggs at once a giant anteater she eats up to 30,000 ants in a single day. The smallest hummingbird move its wings 60-70 times a second. About 3800 species of wasps lives in the United States and Canada, but there are 17000 species worldwide. I don't know who taked the time and had the patience to count eggs, ants, wing beats, and wasps, I'm sure whoever it were needs glasses now.

Corrected Paragraph

A bullfrog can lay 20,000 eggs at once. A giant anteater ~~she~~ eats up to 30,000 ants in a single day. The smallest hummingbird ~~move~~ *moves* its wings 60-70 times a second. About 3,800 species of wasps ~~lives~~ *live* in the United States and Canada, but there are 17,000 species worldwide. I don't know who ~~taked~~ *took* the time and had the patience to count eggs, ants, wing beats, and wasps; *(or)*. I'm sure whoever it ~~were~~ *was* needs glasses now.

WEEK 15: The Galápagos

■ **Using the Right Word, Apostrophe (Possessives), Subject-Verb Agreement, Capitalization, Quotation Marks**

Almost directly South of Guatemala, at the equator, lay the Galápagos islands. The spanish name for these islands are the *Archipiélago de Colón*. Pirates treasures was once hidden there! Today the island group are famous for its reptilian population. Marine iguanas, lizards, and giant tortoises calls it home. The islands are actually named for those tortoises. Galápagos are the Spanish word for turtles.

Corrected Paragraph

Almost directly ~~S~~ *S*outh of Guatemala, at the equator, ~~lay~~ *lie* the Galápagos ~~i~~ *I*slands. The ~~s~~ *S*panish name for these islands ~~are~~ *is* the *Archipiélago de Colón*. Pirates*'* treasures ~~was~~ *were* once hidden there! Today the island group ~~are~~ *is* famous for its reptilian population. Marine iguanas, lizards, and giant tortoises ~~calls~~ *call* it home. The islands are actually named for those tortoises. *"*Galápagos*"* ~~are~~ *is* the Spanish word for turtles.

WEEK 16: **Before Columbus**

■ **Comma (Nonrestrictive Phrases and Clauses and Between Independent Clauses), Period, Sentence Fragment, Apostrophe (Possessives), Wordy Sentence**

Norwegian Vikings sailed west to Iceland, Greenland, and even to the east coast of North America. As early as CE 980, Eric the Red sailed with his family from Iceland to Greenland to settle there. Then his son Leif Ericson who shared his fathers adventuresome spirit. He sailed from Greenland to Vinland the Viking name for the east coast of North America. These daring navigators landed on North America long before Columbus and they established a short-lived settlement there that didn't last very long.

Corrected Paragraph

Norwegian Vikings sailed west to Iceland, Greenland, and even to the east coast of North America. As early as ~~CE~~ *C.E.* 980, Eric the Red sailed with his family from Iceland to Greenland to settle there. Then his son Leif Ericson, who shared his father's adventuresome spirit, He sailed from Greenland to Vinland, the Viking name for the east coast of North America. These daring navigators landed on North America long before Columbus, and they established a short-lived settlement there. ~~that didn't last very long.~~

WEEK 17: The Geography Game

■ **Apostrophe (Possessives), Apostrophe, Comma (Series), Adjective (Articles), Subject-Verb Agreement, Using the Right Word**

Do you has trouble, as I do, remembering wear countries are located and why they are important? Well, heres a neat idea for a geography game. Select a area of the world that you want to no more about. Draw a outline of the area trace out the countries within it and then label and color each country. Next, find out each countrys capitol chief export main industry or major river and writes these on slips of paper. Take turns with an partner, matching countries with the write slips.

Corrected Paragraph

Do you ~~has~~ *have* trouble, as I do, remembering ~~wear~~ *where* countries are located and why they are important? Well, here's a neat idea for a geography game. Select ~~a~~ *an* area of the world that you want to ~~no~~ *know* more about. Draw ~~a~~ *an* outline of the area,/ trace out the countries within it,/ and then label and color each country. Next, find out each country's/ ~~capitol~~ *capital* chief export,/ main industry,/ or major river and ~~writes~~ *write* these on slips of paper. Take turns with ~~an~~ *a* partner, matching countries with the ~~write~~ *right* slips.

WEEK 18: Upside-Down Vision

■ **Comma (To Enclose Information and Nonrestrictive Phrases and Clauses), Spelling, Subject-Verb Agreement, Pronoun-Antecedent Agreement**

Indira Vishnu M.D. told us that human eyes see things upside down. The brain, amazing organ of thought that they are, turns the images right side up agin. The "eye" of a camera also form an inverted image on the film at the back of the camera. Light rays from the top of an object passes through the lens and strikes the lower part of the film. Light rays from the bottom of the object hit the top of the film. This upside-down image which is imprinted on the film appear right side up in the pictures that are diveloped from the negatives.

Corrected Paragraph

Indira Vishnu*/,* M.D.*/,* told us that human eyes see things upside down. The brain, amazing organ of thought that ~~they are~~ *it is*, turns the images right side up ~~agin~~ *again*. The "eye" of a camera also ~~form~~ *forms* an inverted image on the film at the back of the camera. Light rays from the top of an object ~~passes~~ *pass* through the lens and ~~strikes~~ *strike* the lower part of the film. Light rays from the bottom of the object hit the top of the film. This upside-down image*/,*which is imprinted on the film*/,* ~~appear~~ *appears* right side up in the pictures that are ~~diveloped~~ *developed* from the negatives.

WEEK 19: Ancient Survivors

■ **Comma (Addresses and To Separate Adjectives), Subject-Verb Agreement, Adjective (Articles), Colon, Spelling**

Sequoia trees is among the largest and oldest living things on earth. Millions of years ago there were many diffrent kinds, but today only two remain the redwood and the giant sequoia. In Muir Park California giant sequoia trees forms rounded outgrowths along their trunks. These large woody bumps hold tiny seedlings that start to grow if the mother tree is destroyed in an forest fire. This amazing conifer, not surprisingly, are the only one of its species to ensure its survivle in such an manner.

Corrected Paragraph

Sequoia trees ~~is~~ *are* among the largest and oldest living things on earth. Millions of years ago there were many ~~diffrent~~ *different* kinds, but today only two remain: the redwood and the giant sequoia. In Muir Park, California, giant sequoia trees ~~forms~~ *form* rounded outgrowths along their trunks. These large, woody bumps hold tiny seedlings that start to grow if the mother tree is destroyed in ~~an~~ *a* forest fire. This amazing conifer, not surprisingly, ~~are~~ *is* the only one of its species to ensure its ~~survivle~~ *survival* in such ~~an~~ *a* manner.

WEEK 20: **Around and Around**

■ **Comma (Unnecessary and Appositives), Plurals, Pronoun (Reflexive), Rambling Sentence, Italics and Underlining, Spelling**

Copernicus a Polish astronomer who lived in the sixteenth century was the first to suggest, that planets orbit the sun. The later work of Galileo, Kepler, and Newton, confirmed Copernicus' theery of planetary motion. Over the objections of clergymen who taught that the earth was the center of the universe, Copernicus a church official hisself published his theory in a book called On the Revolutions of the Heavenly Spheres, and the book demonstrated the earth's motion in relationship to other heavenly bodys that also moved.

Corrected Paragraph

Copernicus, a Polish astronomer who lived in the sixteenth century, was the first to suggest that planets orbit the sun. The later work of Galileo, Kepler, and Newton confirmed Copernicus' ~~theery~~ *theory* of planetary motion. Over the objections of clergymen who taught that the earth was the center of the universe, Copernicus, a church official ~~hisself~~ *himself* published his theory in a book called <u>On the Revolutions of the Heavenly Spheres</u>. ~~and~~ The book demonstrated the earth's motion in relationship to other heavenly ~~bodys~~ *bodies* that also moved.

WEEK 21: Science Test

■ **Adverb (Comparative/Superlative), Spelling, Nonstandard Language, End Punctuation, Adjective (Comparative/Superlative)**

I stared at the test question: "Why is Earth's gravity more weaker at the equator than anywhere else " I knew that a brick takes longest to fall to the ground at the equator than it takes at the North Pole. But why does it? My mind went completely blank. Altho we had discused this in class, and I could of reviewed my notes, I forgot. Suddenly the answer came to me, and I quickly wrote it out. I was going to ace this one

Corrected Paragraph

I stared at the test question: "Why is Earth's gravity ~~more~~ weaker at the equator than anywhere else?" I knew that a brick takes ~~longest~~ *longer* to fall to the ground at the equator than it takes at the North Pole. But why does it? My mind went completely blank. ~~Altho~~ *Although* we had ~~discused~~ *discussed* this in class, and I could ~~of~~ *have* reviewed my notes, I forgot. Suddenly the answer came to me, and I quickly wrote it out. I was going to ace this one. *(or)* **!**

WEEK 22: Holes in Space

■ **Subject-Verb Agreement, Verb (Irregular), Pronoun (Reflexive), Dash, Adjective (Comparative/Superlative), Quotation Marks, Semicolon**

Some astronomers believe that a black hole is a star that has growed so large and heavy that it has collapsed on it. This results in a body many times smaller and more denser than the original star. Gravitional collapse is another name for this phenomenon. The black hole's gravitational force is so strong that nothing not even light can escape from it. Black holes is invisible scientists try to locate them by measuring the gravitational pull on nearby objects. Talks about finding your way in the dark!

Corrected Paragraph

Some astronomers believe that a black hole is a star that has ~~growed~~ *grown* so large and heavy that it has collapsed on ~~it~~ *itself*. This results in a body many times smaller and ~~more~~ denser than the original star. "Gravitional collapse" is another name for this phenomenon. The black hole's gravitational force is so strong that nothing—not even light—can escape from it. Black holes ~~is~~ *are* invisible; scientists try to locate them by measuring the gravitational pull on nearby objects. ~~Talks~~ *Talk* about finding your way in the dark!

WEEK 23: Leprosy

■ **Comma (Unnecessary and Series), Parentheses, Using the Right Word, Subject-Verb Agreement**

Leprosy or Hansen's disease attacks the skin and causes it too swell and become lumpy and discolored. It can damage nerves weaken hand muscles and create inward-curved fingers. Leprosy was one of the first widespread human diseases; it appeared in India as early as 1500 B.C.E. Its victims was often forced from their homes, and were required to live out their lives away from everyone accept other lepers. This devastating disease, still effects 10 to 15 million people around the world.

Corrected Paragraph

Leprosy (or Hansen's disease) attacks the skin and causes it ~~too~~ *to* swell and become lumpy and discolored. It can damage nerves, weaken hand muscles, and create inward-curved fingers. Leprosy was one of the first widespread human diseases; it appeared in India as early as 1500 B.C.E. Its victims ~~was~~ *were* often forced from their homes, and were required to live out their lives away from everyone ~~accept~~ *except* other lepers. This devastating disease, still ~~effects~~ *affects* 10 to 15 million people around the world.

WEEK 24: True to Yourself

■ **Using the Right Word, Verb (Irregular and Tense), Subject-Verb Agreement, Comma (Appositives), Spelling, Italics and Underlining**

William Shakespeare the famous playwright understood human nature whether he was writing about Roman emperors such as Julius Casear or Danish Kings such as Hamlet. "To thine own self be true" comes from Hamlet a play wrote by William Shakespeare. Parents and teachers have often spoke these words to young people who face dificult decisions. Advice that has stood the test of time for 400 years are probly still true enough too follow. So when your about to make an important dicision in your life, consider all the pros and cons and than do what is right for you!

Corrected Paragraph

William Shakespeare⌃the famous playwright⌃understood human nature
                   ⸝   ⸝
whether he was writing about Roman emperors such as Julius Casear or

Danish Kings such as Hamlet. "To thine own self be true" comes from
                                    written
Hamlet⌃a play ~~wrote~~ by William Shakespeare. Parents and teachers have
       ⸝
      spoken   *difficult*
often ~~spoke~~ these words to young people who face ~~dificult~~ decisions. Advice
                                                is probably
that has stood the test of time for 400 years ~~are~~ ~~probly~~ still true enough
to   *you're*   *decision*
~~too~~ follow. So when ~~your~~ about to make an important ~~dicision~~ in your life,
                                      then
consider all the pros and cons and ~~than~~ do what is right for you!

WEEK 25: Ooooh . . . . Ahh . . . Wow!

■ Comma (Series, To Separate Phrases and Clauses, and Appositives), Capitalization, Verb (Tense), Adjective (Articles), Colon or Dash

Around C.E. 1000 the Chinese invent gunpowder a mixture of saltpeter sulfur and charcoal. They used it for fireworks in national celebrations, such as the birth of a royal child. A eleventh century arabian author referred to the fireworks as "Chinese Snow." Americans use fireworks on the fourth of July to celebrate the birth of their country. They also used fireworks in flares to signal for help or to warn of danger.

Corrected Paragraph

Around C.E. 1000‚ the Chinese ~~invent~~ *invented* gunpowder‚ *(or)* — a mixture of saltpeter‚ sulfur‚ and charcoal. They used it for fireworks in national celebrations, such as the birth of a royal child. ~~A~~ *An* eleventh century ~~a~~*A*rabian author referred to the fireworks as "Chinese Snow." Americans use fireworks on the *F*ourth of July to celebrate the birth of their country. They also ~~used~~ *use* fireworks in flares to signal for help or to warn of danger.

WEEK 26: Two Elizabeths

■ **Using the Right Word, Apostrophe (Possessives), Capitalization, Dash, Comma (To Separate Adjectives)**

Englands queen Elizabeth is the second Elizabeth to rule great Britain. Elizabeth I, born in 1533, was Henry VIII and Anne Boleyns daughter. Elizabeth was one of the strongest most loved and longest-reigning rulers of England. She set on the throne one of Englands most active monarchs for 45 years. Todays monarch has ruled since 1952. That's all ready more than 45 years! She and the first Elizabeth may have more in common then they're names.

Corrected Paragraph

England's *Q*ueen Elizabeth is the second Elizabeth to rule *G*reat Britain. Elizabeth I, born in 1533, was Henry VIII and Anne Boleyn's daughter. Elizabeth was one of the strongest*,* most loved*,* and longest-reigning rulers of England. She ~~set~~ *sat* on the throne — one of England's most active monarchs — for 45 years. Today's monarch has ruled since 1952. That's ~~all ready~~ *already* more than 45 years! She and the first Elizabeth may have more in common ~~then~~ *than* ~~they're~~ *their* names.

WEEK 27: Isn't It Ironic?

■ **Comma (Appositives), Wordy Sentence, Verb (Tense), Spelling, Numbers**

In the 1800s, England wages war against China in order to win the right to sell opium a drug to the Chinese people. However, England outlawed opium at home. Today the United States exported tobacco products to other countries. However, smoking in the United States is "strongly discouraged." 40 years of research have proven over and over again and beyond the shadow of a doubt that smoking is a health hazzard. Does anyone else find these facts ironic?

Corrected Paragraph

In the 1800s, England ~~wages~~ *waged* war against China in order to win the right to sell opium⁄, a drug⁄, to the Chinese people. However, England outlawed opium at home. Today the United States ~~exported~~ *exports* tobacco products to other countries. However, smoking in the United States is "strongly discouraged." ~~40~~ *Forty* years of research have proven ~~over and over~~ ~~again and beyond the shadow of a doubt that~~ smoking is a health ~~hazzard~~ *hazard*. Does anyone else find these facts ironic?

WEEK 28: **Ready or Not**

■ **Comma (Between Independent Clauses), Adjective (Comparative/Superlative), Subject-Verb Agreement, Parallelism, Double Negative**

A toddler who want her freedom may climb a chair to reach a cabinet, chase a ball down a steep stairway, or may be following a kitten into a busy street but someone oldest must stop her before she fall or is injured. Toddlers is too young to understand what Virginia Woolf meant when she wrote, "To enjoy freedom we has to control ourselves." In other words, if we aren't careful, we won't never be *able* to enjoy our freedom!

Corrected Paragraph

A toddler who ~~want~~ *wants* her freedom may climb a chair to reach a cabinet, chase a ball down a steep stairway, or ~~may be following~~ *follow* a kitten into a busy street, but someone ~~oldest~~ *older* must stop her before she ~~fall~~ *falls* or is injured. Toddlers ~~is~~ *are* too young to understand what Virginia Woolf meant when she wrote, "To enjoy freedom we ~~has~~ *have* to control ourselves." In other words, if we aren't careful, we won't ~~never~~ be *able* to enjoy our freedom!

WEEK 29: Words to Live By

■ **Subject-Verb Agreement, Quotation Marks, Run-On Sentence, Spelling, Comma (Dialogue)**

Proverbs is short, popular sayings there are thousands of them. Many proverbs come from ancient times and offen has something to do with common sense. Maybe you've heard someone say "A stitch in time saves nine, or Don't count your chickens before they're hached. These catchy sayings ofer advice and warnings about the hazards of evryday actions.

Corrected Paragraph

Proverbs ~~is~~ *are* short, popular sayings *(or)* **.** *T* ~~there~~ are thousands of them. Many proverbs come from ancient times and ~~offen has~~ *often have* something to do with common sense. Maybe you've heard someone say **,** "A stitch in time saves nine **,**" or "Don't count your chickens before they're ~~hached.~~ *hatched*." These catchy sayings ~~ofer~~ *offer* advice and warnings about the hazards of ~~evryday~~ *everyday* actions.

WEEK 30: Dear Editor:

■ **Using the Right Word, Adverb (Comparative/Superlative), Quotation Marks, Adjective (Articles), Verb (Tense)**

When the teen-center issue came up for a vote by the city counsel, I wrote an letter to the editor and argue for a place where teens could hang out. I wrote, Without a place to go, teens are likelier to find trouble on the streets. I begged for a place where we could have a soda, played games, visit, and listened and danced to our own music. Guess what? The city is planning to build a teen center in a old hardware store at Grand Avenue and Third Street. The pen is mightier then the sword!

Corrected Paragraph

When the teen-center issue came up for a vote by the city ~~counsel~~ *council*, I wrote ~~an~~ *a* letter to the editor and ~~argue~~ *argued* for a place where teens could hang out. I wrote,⸢"⸥ Without a place to go, teens are ~~likelier~~ *more likely* to find trouble on the streets.⸢"⸥ I begged for a place where we could have a soda, ~~played~~ *play* games, visit, and ~~listened~~ *listen* and ~~danced~~ *dance* to our own music. Guess what? The city is planning to build a teen center in ~~a~~ *an* old hardware store at Grand Avenue and Third Street. The pen is mightier ~~then~~ *than* the sword!

WEEK 31: We Love Our Cars

■ **Hyphen (Single-Thought Adjectives), Double Negative, Rambling Sentence, Subject-Verb Agreement, Apostrophe (Possessives)**

Americas love affair with the automobile has caused more than a few problems for our environment. Air pollution may well be the number one problem, but there is others. For example, we throws away 240 to 260 million tires each year—tires that are not never biodegradable and although some companies recycles tires into road surfacing materials, the process are expensive. Another problem is the worlds dwindling supply of petroleum. More earth friendly alternatives must be found so that Americas love affair with cars don't turn into no fatal attraction.

Corrected Paragraph

America's love affair with the automobile has caused more than a few problems for our environment. Air pollution may well be the number one problem, but there ~~is~~ *are* others. For example, we ~~throws~~ *throw* away 240 to 260 million tires each year—tires that are not ~~never~~ biodegradable. ~~and~~ Although some companies ~~recycles~~ *recycle* tires into road-surfacing materials, the process ~~are~~ *is* expensive. Another problem is the world's dwindling supply of petroleum. More earth-friendly alternatives must be found so that America's love affair with cars ~~don't~~ *doesn't* turn into ~~no~~ *a* fatal attraction.

WEEK 32: Cool, Clear Water

■ **Subject-Verb Agreement, Wordy Sentence, Capitalization, Comma (Series), Spelling, Adverb (Comparative/Superlative)**

Some areas of this country faces serious water shortages. An american family of four use almost 200 gallons of water a day for drinking cooking bathing and cleaning. That's 50 gallons per person! One running fausit can send three to five gallons of precious water down the drain every minute. Just one person checking one fausit can make a big difference, and with more people making an effort, conservation would become even more easy. water conservation are everyone's responsability and we should all be doing something about it.

Corrected Paragraph

Some areas of this country ~~faces~~ *face* serious water shortages. An ~~a~~*A*merican family of four ~~use~~ *uses* almost 200 gallons of water a day for drinking*,* cooking*,* bathing*,* and cleaning. That's 50 gallons per person! One running ~~fausit~~ *faucet* can send three to five gallons of precious water down the drain every minute. Just one person checking one ~~fausit~~ *faucet* can make a big difference, and with more people making an effort, conservation would become even ~~more easy~~ *easier*. ~~w~~*W*ater conservation ~~are~~ *is* everyone's ~~responsability~~ *responsibility*. ~~and we should all be doing something about it.~~

WEEK 33: Ban Smog!

■ **Subject-Verb Agreement, Comma (Interjections), Parentheses, Verb (Tense), Capitalization**

In the 1930s, motorists in some midwest cities have to use headlights during the day to see through factory-produced smog. Since then, emissions from America's favorite toy, the automobile, has polluted the air we breathe even more. In 1970, the environmental protection agency EPA was establish to set air-quality standards for industry. Yes we Americans has began to clean up our act, but we still have a long way to go.

Corrected Paragraph

In the 1930s, motorists in some **M**idwest cities ~~have~~ *had* to use headlights during the day to see through factory-produced smog. Since then, emissions from America's favorite toy, the automobile, ~~has~~ *have* polluted the air we breathe even more. In 1970, the **E**nvironmental **P**rotection **A**gency (EPA) was ~~establish~~ *established* to set air-quality standards for industry. Yes, we Americans ~~has began~~ *have begun* to clean up our act, but we still have a long way to go.

WEEK 34: **Breaking Records . . . and Barriers**

■ **Apostrophe, Adjective (Articles), Spelling, Numbers, Combining Sentences, Apostrophe (Possessives)**

Although Jesse Owens, a American track and field athlete, won four gold medals in the 1936 Olympics in Berlin, Germany, Hitler wouldnt shake his hand becaus Owens was black. That only added to Owens fame and glory. Owens set 7 world records in his career. He also worked hard to promote athletics as a natchural arena for equal opportunity. He also promoted athletics as an answer to racial tensions thrughout the world.

Corrected Paragraph

Although Jesse Owens, *an* ~~a~~ American track and field athlete, won four gold medals in the 1936 Olympics in Berlin, Germany, Hitler wouldn't shake his hand *because* ~~becaus~~ Owens was black. That only added to ~~Owens~~ *Owens's (or) Owens'* fame and glory. Owens set *seven* ~~7~~ world records in his career. He also worked hard to promote athletics as a ~~natchural~~ *natural* arena for equal opportunity, ~~He also promoted athletics~~ *and* as an answer to racial tensions *throughout* ~~thrughout~~ the world.

WEEK 35: Batter Up!

■ Comma (Direct Address, To Separate Phrases and Clauses, and Interjections), Numbers, Comma Splice, Adjective (Articles), Spelling

"Maria although good eyes and hands are important they aren't the only requirements for baseball catchers, they need strong leg muscles, too," exsplained the coach. Catchers squat a average of three hundred times during a baseball doubleheader. Wow how's that for some sirius deep knee bends?

Corrected Paragraph

"Maria∧although good eyes and hands are important∧they aren't the
   ,\   ,\
only requirements for baseball catchers,∧they need strong leg muscles, too,"
                                ; (or) ⊙ T
explained
~~exsplained~~ the coach. Catchers squat ~~a~~ *an* average of ~~three hundred~~ *300* times
during a baseball doubleheader. Wow∧how's that for some ~~sirius~~ *serious* deep
                                            ,\
knee bends?

Daily Writing Practice

This section offers three types of exercises. **Writing prompts** are sentences and pictures designed to inspire freewriting (which students may share in class and later shape into finished narratives or essays). **Writing topics** address a wide range of writing ideas. Finally, the **Show-Me sentences** provide practice in developing the important skill of "showing" in writing.

Writing Prompts	**115**
Writing Topics	**139**
Show-Me Sentences	**145**

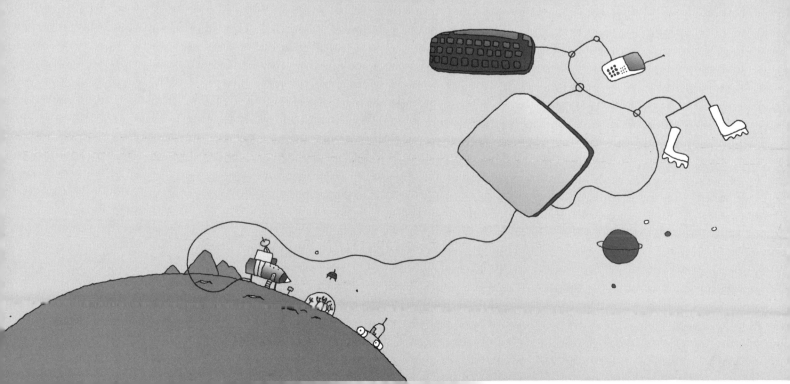

Writing Prompts

A Writing Prompts FAQ Sheet

You may duplicate the following question-and-answer information about writing prompts as a handout for students or use it as the basis for a class discussion.

Anyone who wants to be a good writer has to practice often. That's why so many writers keep journals and diaries. And that's why your teacher asks you to write something nearly every day in school. Your teacher may ask you to write about a specific topic or about a personal experience. Your teacher might also ask you to use a writing prompt.

A writing prompt can be anything from a question to a photograph to a quotation. The idea is for you to write whatever you can without planning or researching the topic. You simply write what you have inside. And you keep writing until all your thoughts are gone. That's it!

How do I get started? It's really very simple. You just write down whatever comes into your mind when you think about your writing prompt. This doesn't have to be much. All you are looking for is an idea to get you going.

Shouldn't I plan out what I'm going to write about? No, you shouldn't plan anything. That's the whole idea. Just write. You don't need to know where your writing will take you. Mystery is good; in fact, it is the mystery and surprises along the way that get writers hooked on writing.

What can I do to keep my writing going? Don't stop! When you run out of ideas, shift gears and try writing about your topic in a slightly different way. For example, you might compare your topic to something else. Or you might invent dialogue between two or more people who are discussing your topic. Or you might think of a specific audience—like a group of first graders—and write so they can understand your topic. Whatever you do, keep the ideas flowing as freely as possible.

When should I stop? If you are doing a timed writing (3, 5, or 10 minutes), stop when the time is up. Otherwise, you might decide it's time to stop when you've filled up the entire page. (Or you might keep going, using another sheet of paper.) Or you might decide to stop when you feel that you've done as much thinking and writing as you can and your brain is drained.

What do I do with my writing? You might share it with a classmate and see what she or he thinks. Or you might turn your writing into a more polished essay, story, or poem. Or you might set it aside and use it later when you need a topic for a writing assignment.

So, really, all I have to do is just start writing? Right!

WRITING PROMPT

It seemed as if time stood still.

_____

_____

_____

_____

_____

_____

_____

_____

_____

_____

_____

_____

_____

_____

_____

_____

_____

_____

WRITING PROMPT
Early one morning . . .

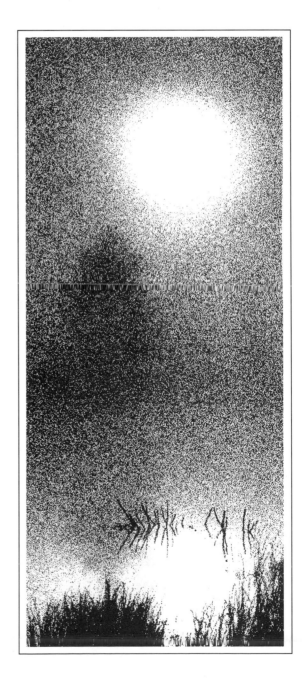

WRITING PROMPT

Sneezing, Itching, Scratching

WRITING PROMPT

I couldn't see a thing!

WRITING PROMPT

It was a terrible storm!

_____

_____

_____

_____

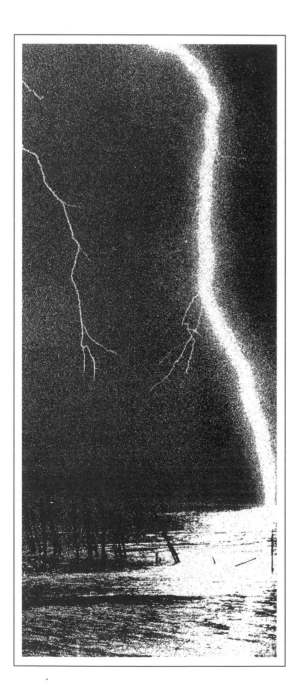

_____

_____

_____

_____

_____

_____

_____

_____

_____

_____

_____

_____

_____

WRITING PROMPT

A place I'd like to visit . . .

WRITING PROMPT
Upside Down

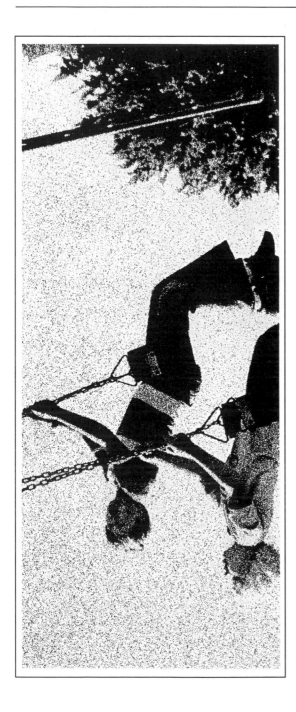

Daily Writing Practice

WRITING PROMPT

What do we do with all this garbage?

WRITING PROMPT

Something I do well (or wish I did) . . .

_____

_____

_____

_____

_____

_____

_____

_____

_____

_____

_____

_____

_____

_____

_____

_____

_____

WRITING PROMPT

What if school sports were dropped?

_____

_____

_____

_____

_____

_____

_____

_____

_____

_____

_____

_____

_____

_____

_____

_____

WRITING PROMPT

If I were very young again . . .

_____

_____

_____

_____

_____

_____

_____

_____

_____

_____

_____

_____

_____

_____

_____

_____

_____

WRITING PROMPT

What do you hear?

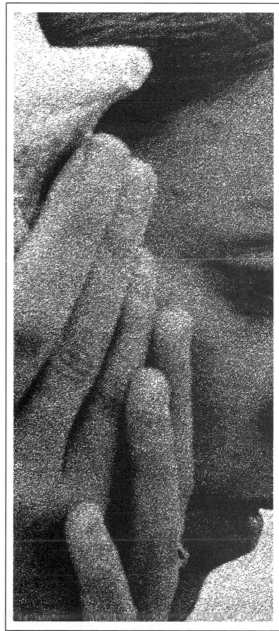

WRITING PROMPT

It's all a blur to me now.

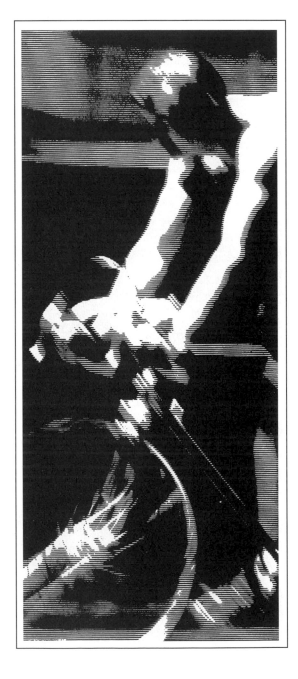

WRITING PROMPT
"Free as a Bird"

WRITING PROMPT

When my parents were my age . . .

_____

_____

_____

_____

_____

_____

_____

_____

_____

_____

_____

_____

_____

_____

_____

_____

WRITING PROMPT

It was very confusing.

WRITING PROMPT

The mind, like a parachute, functions only when open.

_____

_____

_____

_____

_____

_____

_____

_____

_____

_____

_____

_____

_____

_____

WRITING PROMPT

Love is . . .

_____

_____

_____

_____

_____

_____

_____

_____

_____

_____

_____

_____

_____

_____

_____

_____

_____

_____

_____

_____

WRITING PROMPT

It was an experience I'll never forget!

WRITING PROMPT

What Freedom Means to Me

_____

_____

_____

_____

_____

_____

_____

_____

_____

_____

_____

_____

_____

_____

_____

_____

_____

WRITING PROMPT

Twilight's calm . . .

_____

_____

_____

_____

_____

_____

_____

_____

_____

_____

_____

_____

_____

_____

_____

_____

_____

_____

WRITING PROMPT
A Trip to the Mall

_____

_____

_____

_____

_____

_____

_____

_____

_____

_____

_____

_____

_____

_____

_____

_____

_____

Writing Topics
Daily Journal Writing

> "I can tap into [my students'] human instincts to write if I help them realize that their lives and memories are worth telling stories about, and if I help them zoom in on topics of fundamental importance to them."
>
> —writing teacher June Gould

We provided our students with four or five personal writing topics each time they wrote. They could use one of these topics as a starting point, or write about something else entirely. The choice was theirs. (We found that providing writing topics was much easier and more productive than going into our "You've got plenty to write about" song and dance.)

As classroom teachers, we know from firsthand experience that the personal stories young learners love to share can serve as the basis of an effective and lively writing program. Here's how we did it:

Getting Started

At the beginning of the school year, we introduced in-class journal writing to the students. (We encouraged students to write outside of class in journals as well, but the journals in school were part of our writing program.) We knew that the most effective way to get students into writing was simply to let them write often and freely about their own lives, without having to worry about grades or turning their writing in. This helped them develop a feel for "real" writing— writing that originates from their own thoughts and feelings.

That's where the journals come in. Nothing gets a student into writing more effectively than a personal journal. (And no other type of writing is so easy to implement.) All your students need are spiral notebooks, pens, time to write, and encouragement to explore whatever is on their minds. (See page 145 in the *Write Source 2000* handbook for more information.)

Writing Topics

To start off an exercise, we posted a list of suggested writing topics like these:

- your most memorable kitchen-related experience,
- coping with younger brothers or sisters,
- being home alone, late at night, or
- what you did over the past weekend.

Students would either choose from the list or write about a topic they preferred. See pages 141-145 for more suggested topics.

We asked our students to write every other day for the first 10 minutes of the class period. (Monday, Wednesday, and Friday were writing days.) Of course, we had to adjust our schedule at times, but, for the most part, students wrote three times a week.

Keeping It Going

After everyone was seated and roll was taken, the journals were passed out, the topics were given, and everyone wrote. We expected students to write for a full 10 minutes, nonstop. And we made sure that they did. They knew that they would earn a quarterly journal grade based on the number of words they produced. This almost made a contest out of the writing sessions. Each time they wrote, they wanted to see if they could increase their production from past journal entries, and they always wanted to write more than their classmates.

> "Over the last fifteen years, a number of teachers around the country and their students have been amazed by what happened when people write ten to fifteen minutes without worrying about grammar, spelling, or punctuation, and concentrating only on telling some kind of truth."
>
> —Ken Macrorie

Wrapping It Up

On days that we weren't writing, we shared journal entries. First, each student exchanged journals with a classmate. He or she would count the number of words in the latest entry, read it carefully, and then make comments on things he or she liked or questioned. After each pair had shared their comments with one another, we talked about the entries as a class.

Many writers were reluctant to share their entries with the entire group. But the readers had no problem volunteering someone else's entry ("You've got to hear Nick's story") and reading it out loud. The students loved these readings and the discussions that followed.

Personal Experience Papers

Periodically, we would interrupt the normal course of journal writing and make formal writing assignments. That is, we would ask students to review their entries and select one (or part of one) to develop into a more polished, complete personal experience paper. Usually, those entries that readers had enjoyed and wanted to know more about would be the ones the young writers chose to develop.

We wanted to make sure that their writing went through at least one or two thorough revisions, so we gave our writers plenty of class time to work on their papers. We also required them to turn in all preliminary work with their final drafts. (See "Autobiographical Writing," page 153, in the *Write Source 2000* handbook for guidelines for this type of writing.)

The experience papers were shared with the entire class at the end of the project. This was a fun and informal activity, but one that students came to appreciate as an important part of the entire composing process. It was their day. They were on stage. They were sharing the culmination of all their hard work—a special moment in their own lives.

Writing Topics

The topics on the following pages can be used as daily writing prompts for journal or personal writing.

Friends

- Staying at a friend's house
- Cliques in my school
- What if we suddenly had to move?
- A typical phone call goes like this.
- My first friend
- What to look for in a friend
- A visit to a friend's house/school
- Hanging out

Memories

- A holiday I'll never forget
- My worst/best vacation
- A "visit" to a hospital/doctor's office
- Talk about being scared!
- Putting my foot in my mouth
- My muscles were so sore . . .
- Suddenly I realized the truth: I was lost!
- My first concert
- I'll never eat another . . .
- It caused a big lump in my throat.

Who am I?

- Who knows me best?
- My life story begins this way.
- What should everyone know about me?
- My best day ever
- My worst day
- My bedroom from top to bottom
- My secret snacks
- My chores
- What I like/don't like about my class schedule
- The possessions I feel are most worth keeping
- What makes me mad? happy? sad? worried? scared?
- Where do I fit in?
- Do I want to be famous?
- The toys/games I'll never give up
- If I were someone else, I'd be . . .
- Sometimes I take things too seriously (or not seriously enough).

Writing Topics

Making Decisions

- A narrow escape from trouble

- If only I would have done that differently.

- If only I would have listened!

- It's my turn to buy the family groceries for the week. Here's my shopping list.

- What are some of life's most useful objects?

- Where do I draw the line?

- Which is more valuable— wealth or a good job?

- What if I could skip a grade?

Food for Thought

- "Someone who makes no mistakes does not usually make anything."

- "When people are free to do as they please, they usually imitate each other."

- "Everybody is ignorant, only on different subjects."

- "Obstacles are what you see when you take your mind off your goal."

- "Progress makes us lazy."

- "Life is like a sandwich; the more you add to it, the better it becomes."

Being Creative

- Here's a look at the next episode of "As the School Swings."

- It may sound crazy, but . . .

- One day I woke up late and . . .

- Here's what I find interesting about people.

- Whenever I hear (a song), I think of . . .

- If I could step back in time, I'd like to . . .

- Why do people keep journals or diaries?

- What if I had to produce most of my own food?

- What if I never forgot?

- If I could wear whatever I wanted . . .

- What if all teachers taught different subjects and grade levels every year?

- I wish I had invented . . .

- If I could be any place . . .

Writing Topics

School Daze

- Here's what a new student needs to know about my school.

- I'm principal for the day. Here's my schedule of events.

- A typical lunch period

- A difficult practice/assignment

- A memorable ride on a school bus

- My best class ever

- I was so embarrassed I wanted to hide in my locker.

- What this school really needs is . . .

- How important are grades?

- Progress reports/report cards

- I memorized every word.

- What makes school "exciting"?

- Our school mascot

- The animal our school building resembles is . . .

- After-school sports

- Field trips

- Crossing guards

- My first day in this school

- My best (or worst) day with a substitute

- Science lab adventure

- Between classes

- The view from my classroom

- Our class (or school) newspaper

- An unforgettable classroom visitor

- Snow days

- The best musical event of the year

- Classroom pets

- The biggest mystery in our school

- The funniest school assembly

- The best group I ever worked with

Writing Topics

At the Edge

- It takes courage to . . .

- Courageous people I know

- Exploring the wilderness

- Fast roller coasters

- Rafting on white water

- Someday I'd like to . . .

- The life of a pioneer

- Rock climbing

- Surviving camp

Choices

- May I have this dance?

- Your clothes say something about you.

- Why are people vegetarians?

- My favorite kind of music

- Boys and girls should be allowed to participate in all school sports.

- The movies I want to see

Animals

- The best pet for city dwellers

- Taking good care of pets

- Watchdogs

- Hunting is/is not a sport

- A dog is a person's best friend.

- Animals trained to help people

- Medical experiments on animals

- The reason for zoos

- Wild animals

Books

- You have to read . . .

- My favorite place to read

- A book I'll never forget

- I loved listening to this book read aloud.

- Authors I like

- Book characters that I'd like to meet

Show-Me Sentences
Producing Writing with Detail

From time immemorial, teachers have said to their students, "Your essay lacks details" or "This idea is too general" or "Show, don't tell." We even know of a teacher who had a special stamp made: "Give more examples."

So how should this writing problem be approached? It's obvious that simply telling students to add more details and examples is not enough. Even showing them how professional writers develop their ideas is not enough (although this does help). Students learn to add substance and depth to their writing through regular practice.

Here's one method that has worked for many students and teachers: *Show-Me* sentences. Students begin with a basic topic—"My locker is messy," for example—and create a paragraph or brief essay that *shows* rather than *tells*. The sentence is a springboard for lively writing.

About Your Show-Me Sentences

The following pages contain 45 Show-Me sentences. Each sentence speaks directly to middle-school students, so they should have little difficulty creating essays full of personal details. Again, we suggest that you use these sentences every other day for an extended period of time (at least a month).

Note: By design, each page of Show-Me sentences can be made into an overhead transparency.

Implementation

DAY ONE Before you ask students to work on their own, develop a Show-Me sentence as a class. Start by writing a sample sentence on the board. Then have students volunteer specific details that give this basic thought some life. List their ideas on the board. Next, construct a brief paragraph on the board using some of these details. (Make no mention of the original sentence in your paragraph.) Discuss the results. Make sure that your students see how specific details help create a visual image for the reader. Also have your students read and react to examples of "showing writing" from professional texts. (Share the model on page 147 with your students.)

DAY TWO Have students work on their first Show-Me sentences in class. Upon completion of their writing, have pairs of students share the results of their work. Then ask for volunteers to share their writing with the entire class. (Make copies of strong writing for future class discussions.)

DAY THREE Ask students to develop a new paragraph. At the beginning of the *next* class period, discuss the results (break into pairs as before). Continue in this fashion for at least a month.

Note: Reserve the first 10 or 15 minutes of each class period for writing or discussing. (Students who don't finish their writing in class should have it ready for the next day.)

Evaluation

Students should reserve a section in their notebooks for their writing or compile their work in a folder. At regular intervals, give them some type of performance score for their efforts. At the end of the unit, have them select one or two of their best examples to revise and submit for a thorough evaluation.

Enrichment

For additional work in this area, refer to *Writers in Training* by Rebekah Caplan (Dale Seymour Publications, 1984). Ms. Caplan has developed an extensive program to help students produce well-detailed, engaging essays. She makes the following suggestions:

● Have your students turn cliches like *It's a small world* or *Accidents will happen* into strong narrative or descriptive paragraphs.

● Have them develop sentences like *Friday nights are better than Saturday nights* into paragraphs that compare and contrast two subjects.

● In addition, have students convert loaded statements like *Noon hours are too short* or *I don't need a curfew* into opinion pieces.

Note: In a sense, these variations become progressively more challenging. Most student writers, for example, have more difficulty supporting an opinion than they have illustrating the basic ideas behind a cliche.

● You might also use vocabulary words in Show-Me sentences or connect these sentences to literary works under study. (Generally speaking, Show-Me sentences can be linked to any unit of study.)

(Please refer to *Writers in Training* for more information about each of these ideas.)

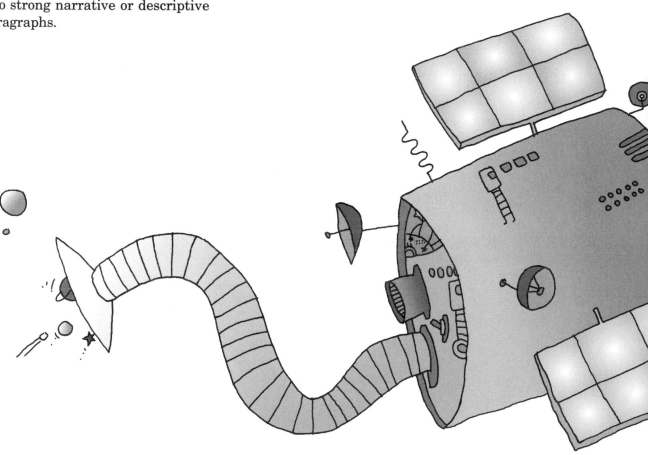

Sample Writing

My baby sister was the picture of health.
(cliche)

Josie flitted from one thing to another, as if everything in the kitchen were there for her amusement. She had already left a trail of pots, pans, bananas, and crackers behind her. Flashing Mom a bright-eyed smile, she reached her dimpled hands toward her juice cup. The juice dribbled down her chin as she drank. A swipe across her plump cheeks with her hand took care of that. She plunked the half-empty cup on the counter and started to sing to herself as she marched around the kitchen table. A sound from the yard suddenly caught her attention, and she ran toward the back door on eager little legs.

SHOW-ME SENTENCES

My room was messy.

She (he) is nice.

The game was a disaster.

Study hall is a waste of time.

She (he) works hard.

SHOW-ME SENTENCES

The play was a blast.

I hate winter mornings.

I love Saturday mornings.

The weather changed.

I was in charge.

SHOW-ME SENTENCES

Our dog is one of a kind.

I'm not a morning person.

The drive-in was crowded.

She (he) went crazy.

Ms. (Mr.) _____ is so funny.

SHOW-ME SENTENCES

The local news (newspaper) is pretty dull.

Our last school assembly was interesting, to say the least.

Lunchtime is always an adventure.

I (he, she) take things too seriously.

Her (his) bark is worse than her (his) bite.

SHOW-ME SENTENCES

She (he) is a worrywart.

I didn't think I'd ever get out of that class.

A chill ran down my spine.

We proved that might is not always right.

They are as different as night and day.

SHOW-ME SENTENCES

Did she ever put her foot in her mouth!

It was as easy as one, two, three.

You could hear a pin drop.

He always ends up on the wrong end of the stick.

I'm up to here with _____ .

SHOW-ME SENTENCES

Two's company, and three's a crowd.

She (he) has created a real storm.

The _____ think they're cool.

Sixth graders are different from seventh graders.

My next-door neighbor is different from my mother (father).

SHOW-ME SENTENCES

It was an unforgettable bike ride.

There is no such thing as a typical day in our _____ class.

Our field trip to _____ was interesting.

Many TV commercials are misleading.

Doing my chores is no picnic.

SHOW-ME SENTENCES

I have fun on weekends.

Performing stunt-bike tricks can be dangerous.

Her hairdo is wild.

My leg really hurt when I broke it.

I enjoyed the last week of summer vacation.